NHS BLACKPOOL HEALTH PROFESSIONALS' LIBRARY

KT-556-095

A career in medicine:
do you have what it takes?

The Blackpool, Fylde & Wyre
Health Library

This book is due for return on or before the last date shown below
to avoid overdue charges.
Books may be renewed (twice only) unless required by other readers.
Renewals may be made in person or by telephone, quoting reader number
and the number on the barcode below.

BLACKPOOL, FYLDE AND WYRE
NHS LIBRARY

TV11154

A career in medicine: do you have what it takes?

Edited by

Harvey White DM MCh FRCS

The ROYAL
SOCIETY *of*
MEDICINE
PRESS *Limited*

©2000 Royal Society of Medicine Press Ltd
1 Wimpole Street, London W1G 0AE, UK
207 E Westminster Road, Lake Forest, IL 60045, USA
http://www.roysocmed.ac.uk

Apart from any fair dealing for the purposes of research or private study, criticism
or review, as permitted under the UK Copyright Designs and Patents Act, 1988, no
part of this publication may be reproduced, stored or transmitted, in any form or
by any means, without the prior permission in writing of the publishers or in the case
of reprographic reproduction in accordance of the terms of licences issued by the
Copyright Licensing Agency in the UK, or in accordance with the terms of licences
issued by the appropriate Reproduction Rights Organization outside the UK.
Enquiries concerning reproduction outside the terms stated here should be sent to
the publishers at the UK address printed on this page.

This book is published by the Royal Society of Medicine Press Ltd. The contributors
are responsible for the content and for the views expressed, which are not
necessarily those of the editor, of the Royal Society of Medicine or of the Royal
Society of Medicine Press Ltd.

British Library Cataloguing in Publication Data
A catalogue record for this book is available from the British Library
ISBN 1-85315-462-8

Phototypeset by Phoenix Photosetting, Chatham, Kent, UK
Cartoons by GH Graphics, Charing, Kent, UK
Printed in Great Britain by Ebenezer Baylis, The Trinity Press, Worcester, UK

610.690941 WHI

Contributors

Editor

Mr Harvey White
Consulting Surgeon, Royal Marsden Hospital, London

Authors

Dr Robina Coker
Senior Lecturer and Honorary Consultant in Respiratory Medicine,
Hammersmith Hospital, London

Professor Raanan Gillon
Emeritus Professor of Medical Ethics, Imperial College of Science,
Technology and Medicine, London

Mr Kevin Lafferty
Consultant Surgeon, Basildon Hospital, Essex

Nick Loman
Student, St Bartholomew's and the Royal London School of Medicine and
Dentistry, London

Professor David Lowe
Assistant Warden for Admissions, St Bartholomew's and the Royal London
School of Medicine and Dentistry, London

Dr Elisabeth Paice
Dean Director of Postgraduate Medical & Dental Education, North
Thames, London

Dr Edward Shaoul
Associate Dean, GP Regional Postgraduate Dean's Office, St Charles'
Hospital, London

Professor John Stein
Lecturer in Physiology, Magdalen College, Oxford

Professor Eric Thomas
Dean, Faculty of Medicine, Health and Biological Sciences, University of Southampton, Southampton

Dr Simon Thorn
Head of Biology, Radley College, Abingdon, Oxfordshire

Dr Marcus Wagstaff
Senior House Officer in Surgery, Queen's Medical Centre, Nottingham

About the editor

Having been at school at Winchester College, Harvey White graduated from Magdalen College, University of Oxford in 1961. He obtained a Doctorate in Medicine (DM) and Mastership in Surgery (MCh) from Oxford and the Fellowship of the Royal College of Surgeons (FRCS) in 1970. He worked as a Senior Registrar at St Bartholomew's Hospital, London where he had also been a clinical student and a lecturer in physiology for five years. He was Consultant Surgeon at the Royal Marsden Hospital from 1976 where he was Chairman of the Division of Surgery and remains an honorary Consulting Surgeon. He has been a Consultant Surgeon at King Edward VII Hospital for Officers since 1983 and was Hunterian Professor at the Royal College of Surgeons in 1988.

Over the years he has served as Secretary and Vice-President of the British Association of Surgical Oncology, President of the Medical Society of London, a member of the Cancer Relief Macmillan Council and, since 1986, Chairman of the Brendoncare Foundation for the Elderly.

In addition to his work on medical committees, he has contributed many articles and chapters to surgical journals and books as well as editing specialized surgical books and journals including *Clinical Oncology* and the *European Journal of Surgical Oncology*. More recently, he has contributed to works on the History of Medicine and Surgery including *The Oxford Companion to Medicine*.

Having previously served as Honorary Editor at the Royal Society of Medicine, he has been Chairman of the Royal Society of Medicine Press for the past three years.

Contents

Preface

A few years ago, I felt there was a need for potential medical students at school to focus on how they could best achieve their ambitions. An annual medical careers day for sixth form students held at the Royal Society of Medicine has since been set up and has proved to be a popular and worthwhile event. I thought it would be useful to publish a book based on the meetings.

This highly informative book includes chapters written by experts in their field, beginning with an analysis of who should pursue a career in medicine; it then discusses in detail the entry requirements, interview techniques, and useful hints for choosing a medical school, medical career and subsequent specialization. In addition, there are chapters on ethical issues, the options of general practice (primary care) and hospital medicine, and an insight into both the student and resident years.

The success and value of this book is entirely dependent on the enthusiasm of those who have contributed to it. It has been compiled as a record for those who attend the meeting, for those attending in the future and for those unable to attend who might benefit from the excellent contributions.

The wisdom and interest of the participants has been a great inspiration to those who arranged the symposium. This book is dedicated to all those who are now on the threshold of their careers. The Academic Dean of the Royal Society of Medicine, Dr Jack Tinker, has been especially supportive and helpful with planning the annual meeting, and I am very grateful to him.

Harvey White
Chairman of the Royal Society of Medicine Press Ltd
Consultant Surgeon, London

Why choose a career in medicine?

Professor Eric Thomas, *Dean, University of Southampton Medical School*

Sigmund Freud, the Austrian psychiatrist, said: 'Life is to love and work'.

People spend so much of their waking time working that it is essential to find a career that is truly absorbing and satisfying. Medicine fulfils these criteria completely.

Reasons for becoming a doctor

There are many reasons for choosing a career in medicine. A few are listed below.

◎ Medicine helps people and society. You will be a useful person at an individual and collective level.

◎ Medicine addresses issues of importance. In your individual interactions with people you will be addressing issues of prime concern to them. You will be privileged to be present at births and deaths, and at many other occasions — sad and happy — in between.

◎ Medicine offers a major intellectual challenge. It does not just require ordinary intelligence, but a more rounded, emotional intelligence. You will need to use your brain to communicate, to interact, to learn and relearn different skills.

◎ Medicine confronts important moral and ethical issues, ie when to treat, designer babies, withdrawal of life support, euthanasia, and genetics — all these issues have a strong ethical dimension.

◎ Medicine is fun! You will join a 'tribe' with its own set of values and behaviours. Much teamwork is involved, and most doctors develop a good sense of humour.

◎ Medicine is extremely varied. It is not just a monochrome career — within the same profession, you can choose to be an academic researcher, a general practitioner (GP), a pathologist, a television doctor, a medical journalist and a host of other options.

◎ Medicine is secure and well paid. Although salaries are not at the level of city traders, GPs earning about £50,000/year and consultants

> *Medicine is fun! You will join a 'tribe' with its own set of values and behaviours*

about £60–70,000 (somewhat more with private practice) are still in the top 2% of income earners in the UK.

- Medicine offers a mobile qualification. You can travel to Australia, the US, Canada, Europe or the Far East. European law allows you to work anywhere in the European Union. Academic research can take you to Stanford, Harvard or Melbourne; or you can use your skills for the benefit of less developed countries in Voluntary Service Overseas, or with groups such as Médicins sans Frontières.

- Journey into yourself — it will be challenging. You will have to face grief, loss and unhappiness as well as their opposites. Medicine is a career that will challenge and entertain you throughout your life.

Possible reasons for not becoming a doctor

Some people may not be suited to a medical career. A few reasons why they should not pursue this profession are listed below.

- Medicine requires good social and communication skills. It will not suit those who do not much enjoy being with people.
- Medicine is very hard work — but so is any other job worth doing. Barristers and business people work equally long hours.
- Medicine is stressful and demanding. Doctors have higher levels of mental illness than the general population.
- Your career can peak very early. You can be a qualified GP at the age of 28 or 29 years, or a consultant in hospital medicine in your mid-30s. In other careers, people carry on developing into their 40s and 50s. Doctors can become bored or frustrated if they do not see any progression beyond that early endpoint.

Conclusion

Overall, however, medicine is a wonderful and challenging career. I have never regretted the choice. It has given me wall-to-wall enjoyment, and I do not see why it should not do the same for you!

Entry requirements for medical school 2

*Professor **John Stein**, Medical Tutor, Magdalen College, Oxford University*

This chapter aims to help you obtain a place at a medical school, focusing on the qualities and qualifications needed for this profession. The degree of your commitment to medicine is so important, not only for achieving a place at medical school but also for determining whether or not you will enjoy this career afterwards, that you need to think very carefully about whether or not you really want to study it at all. If, having examined yourself and your motivations thoroughly and honestly, the pros do not easily outweigh the cons of medicine for you, then I earnestly entreat that you consider another career.

Important qualities in a doctor

The ideal doctor should be:

◎   knowledgeable
◎   compassionate and sensitive to people's feelings
◎   altruistic
◎   eager to help people and to make a difference to their lives
◎   dedicated and hard working, with the highest integrity
◎   reasonably intelligent, with a retentive memory and an enquiring mind
◎   interested in how the body works
◎   an articulate and sensitive communicator with very high personal standards of morality
◎   full of energy, with good organizational skills and able to work in a highly interdependent team
◎   tolerant, not only of long hours and hard physical labour but also capable of coping with sometimes horrifying emotional traumas.

Such saints do not, of course, exist in real life but this is what we aspire to — these ideals dictate what *you* should be looking for in yourself. The most important general quality a doctor should have is a liking for and an interest in people, even the difficult ones. You really need to enjoy interacting and

> *You should enjoy interacting and empathizing with all ranks, shapes, cultures, classes and religions*

empathizing with all ranks, shapes, cultures, classes and religions, even those who try to insult and humiliate you.

Modern medicine involves the exciting application of scientific principles to help people by counteracting the cruel hereditary, environmental, social and random determinants of disease. Thus, you must not only have a genuine interest in human physiology, in how muscles contract, how smoking causes lung cancer and how high blood pressure causes kidney problems, but also in why American Indians are intolerant to alcohol and why low-income groups have an increased burden of disease, and why this affects not only themselves but sadly even their unborn children.

Good practical skills and team player

You should also be a very practical person and enjoy using your hands. Eliciting physical signs, feeling for an enlarged liver, listening to heart murmurs and testing muscle reflexes are as important for making a correct diagnosis and deciding on an appropriate course of treatment as listening to your patient's history and account of the symptoms. Moreover, if you specialize in fields such as surgery, anaesthesia or modern interventional radiology, you will need to develop even greater practical skills.

Another increasingly important quality is the ability to work in a team. The kind, single-handed practitioner who looked after your grandparents with little help from anyone else is a concept of the past. Medicine today depends on teamwork, and although the head of the team is usually a doctor, that is by no means always the case. Whatever the situation, you are interdependent — the surgeon depends on the anaesthetist and theatre nurse, who both depend on the theatre cleaner to maintain asepsis. Afterwards, both patient and surgeon depend on the physiotherapist to get limbs moving again. All these people depend on the hospital managers who try to ensure that the money is distributed evenly so that everybody and everything is in the right place at the right time. Thus, in order to work successfully, a doctor should be good at communicating with many different kinds of people, who form a team delivering care.

Flexible and dedicated approach to work

You must enjoy a life of great variety and change. There is very little predictable routine in medicine; the practice of medicine is changing all the time and will change much more with the advent of individually tailored approaches derived from molecular genetics. Moreover, there are frequent moments of great stress. You must not 'lose your head' at such times. You will have no more than three or four minutes to restart the heart when your patient collapses with ventricular fibrillation; so you cannot afford your mind to go blank while you panic about what to do. If you find the thought of such change, unpredictability and crisis disturbing, you may be better off thinking of another career.

Medicine is almost a 24-hour occupation. It is hard work physically due to the long hours that are involved — heart attacks seldom conveniently resolve at 5 pm. It is also emotionally demanding as you are in the privileged position of taking responsibility for other people's lives. A corollary of your compassionate and sensitive empathy with your patients is a crushing sense of failure when on occasion they die, despite your best efforts.

As you will not have enough experience in the first 10 years of your medical career, you may feel that you are at the bottom of a hierarchy that could make you feel small and undervalued; this aspect of professional life, however, is improving rapidly. In addition, the five-year medical course is one of the longest and involves a lot of hard work but you must not forget that, by the time you are fully qualified, the state will have spent about £200,000 on training you.

So you must be sure that the drawbacks of medicine do not outweigh its advantages for you. How strongly you judge the arguments in favour of a career in medicine depends on you and your character. To make up your mind, you must obtain as much information as you can about what medicine is really like by shadowing doctors, attending clinics or helping in hospitals. If you can, make a point of talking to junior doctors, as they see medicine at its toughest.

If you find it appealing to be able to help people at their most vulnerable, to make a real difference to their lives and eventually to become your own master when making life or death decisions, you will find medicine infinitely rewarding and fulfilling, and well worth the sacrifice of time and effort. You will gain gratitude, respect, status and trust from your patients and your peers. Also, you will seldom be unemployed and your salary will be reasonably good and reliable. If you feel you may resent the time and effort that will have to be spent, and the way in which medicine can dominate your life, do not do medicine.

Necessary qualifications

If you are convinced, after thorough and honest weighing up of the above considerations, that you want to apply to read medicine, then you must maximize your chances of obtaining an entry place. To obtain a place at the medical school of your choice, you must organize your campaign well and start as early as possible. The first thing is to be realistic about how highly competitive this is. About two-and-a-half people apply for each of the current 8,000 places/year available at British medical schools. As each person has four choices this can look far worse, so that the current favourite, the University of Nottingham Medical School, has more than 20 candidates for each place. Choosing the best medical school for you is discussed in chapter 5, but it is important that you visit as many as you can and talk to the students there as they will give you the best idea of what the place is really like.

General Certificate of Secondary Education (GCSE) level

If you can, you need to achieve a high number of A and A' grades at GCSE level. Your GCSEs are the only public examination results by which selection panels can judge you. Also, they are known to predict university degree performance — in fact rather better than A levels, for it is not so easy to 'cram'. Selectors pay much attention to GCSE results; some medical schools even state that they will not consider anybody with less than four grade As at GCSE unless there are special circumstances. You will usually need to have passed at least mathematics, physics, chemistry, biology, English and a language other than English, eg Welsh, French or Spanish. Dual award science will usually substitute for physics, chemistry and biology, but not mathematics.

Universities and College Admissions System (UCAS) form

Selectors will pay as much attention to your personal statement as to your examination record and school report. In your personal statement, you must

try to communicate your genuine interest in medicine and your desire to help people in need. Everyone involved in the health service wants to help people, so you must demonstrate your intelligence, responsibility, energy and enthusiasm to become a doctor, and that you know what that actually means. You must show that you have practical experience of what doctors do and have thought realistically about the life that medicine entails through work experience or other attachments.

Interviewers also like to see a wide variety of other interests, not because oarsmen, actresses or pianists necessarily make better doctors, but because carrying out any of these to a high standard at the same time as achieving high academic success demonstrates your broader horizons and your ability to organize yourself sufficiently well to find time to do both. Practice writing all this down in several versions and ask other people to comment on it before committing yourself to the actual UCAS form.

Your school report should make the same points, reinforcing your account of your past and potential future achievements, eg academic, sporting, cultural, political or social. It should also provide evidence of your having thought deeply about medicine as a career, by experiencing it first hand through work experience etc; your teacher should give an opinion and further evidence about how committed you are to a career in medicine.

A levels

The main thing your school report will contain is the school's predictions of your A level grades, which currently need to be a minimum of ABB unless there are exceptional reasons for lower grades. As for the subjects you should choose, the only essential is chemistry because so much of physiology, biochemistry, pharmacology and molecular pathology depend on a knowledge of chemical reactions and their mechanisms. One other science or mathematics is usually needed, but biology at A level is not essential if you have it or dual award science at GCSE. Those who have studied physical sciences and mathematics at A level are, thus, welcomed by most medical schools. Of course, you must also be seriously interested in medicine. One thing that this often means in practice is that you will be asked in the interview how you think your knowledge of the physical sciences will help you in your medical studies and thereafter. You should have thought carefully and acquired some knowledge about how the subjects that you have studied relate to medicine. Many very successful doctors studied the physical sciences at A level and were not impeded at all by the absence of biology knowledge at that stage. Selectors, including myself, find that, after a few weeks of becoming familiar with the nomenclature of medical science much of which is borrowed from biology, those who have studied the physical sciences progress just as quickly as the biologists.

Most medical schools now require only two sciences at A level, but some are even happy with only chemistry. This means that you are encouraged to take an arts subject at A level if you wish to, and this will not disadvantage you in any way. This change has arisen as we now place more emphasis on the importance of the doctor's ability to communicate successfully with patients from all walks of life. Study of an arts subject should not only cultivate your literacy skills but it should also broaden your mind to other cultures and classes, and other ways of thinking and communicating.

Gap year

Most medical schools are now happy if you want to take a year out between school and university to travel, as long as your proposed programme is constructive, eg visiting countries with interesting medical problems or doing a useful job and not just lazing around at home or going to parties. Conversely, you may feel that you want to do something entirely different from medicine to broaden your experience of the world. You might feel you would be more useful in a hospital or clinic once you have almost completed your course. You will be encouraged to spend your elective period (the opportunity to work as a junior doctor in another country) in the second or third clinical training years working in a third world medical clinic, and may decide that this is where you will eventually be more useful in a medical capacity.

Graduates

Most medical schools take a small number of graduates from other subjects to read medicine. Some accelerated, fast-track graduate courses that last only four years have recently been introduced for those who have previously obtained a science honours degree. Given the competition for undergraduate places, however, it is not realistic to attempt to change to medicine unless you have or expect to achieve at least a 2(i) class in your first degree. Some universities also provide a few places for a pre-medical conversion course — often termed first Bachelor of Medicine (MB) — which covers basic chemistry, biology, mathematics and physics for those who have previously studied entirely arts subjects. Often, however, it

is only necessary to take A level chemistry to qualify for consideration.

Your interviewers will be concentrating on assessing the strength of your commitment to medicine. The obvious question is, 'If you are now so keen on studying medicine, why didn't you apply from school?' An honest answer would often be, 'I wasn't sure then, and anyway I didn't get good enough A levels'. Hence, you would have to be able to explain the latter, and convince the panel that you are now totally committed to medicine.

> *To obtain a place at medical school, you need to organize your campaign well*

Summary

You should spend time investigating what medicine is really like at the coal face and start thinking about how you would react to those conditions. Talk to doctors, particularly junior ones who can tell you what they find good and bad about their lives. Be brutally honest in the examination of your character — do not confuse what you think you should be like with what, in your heart of hearts, you know you are really like.

If you still want to devote your life to medicine after all this introspection, you must try to obtain good GCSE results and study appropriate A level subjects — at least chemistry and perhaps an arts subject — aiming for ABB grades or higher. In your personal statement, try to communicate your particular reasons for being enthusiastic about medicine, your ability to work in a team, and demonstrate your intelligence, energy, wide interests and organizational skills. Ensure that the teacher who writes your school report reinforces your claims.

Further reading

Visit the websites of the medical schools to which you are going to apply.
British Medical Association website: http://www.bma.org.uk.

Becoming a doctor. London: BMA publications, 1999.

British Medical Association. *Medical careers — a general guide*. London: BMJ Publishing Group,1994. (ISBN 0727910876)

Richards P, Stockill S. *Learning medicine*. London: BMJ Publishing Group, 2000. (ISBN 0727914626)

Corps L, Urmston I. *The insiders guide to medical schools (the alternative prospectus) 1999*. London: BMJ Publishing Group, 1999. (ISBN 0727914286)

Rushton J. *Getting into medical school*. London: Troutman & Company Ltd, 1998.

Houghton A, Gray D. *Getting into medicine: so you want to be a doctor*. London: Hodder & Stoughton Publishers, 1997. (ISBN 0340701587)

Hopkins D. *So you want to be a doctor? (An insider's guide to a medical career).* London: Kogan Page, 1998. (ISBN 0749427868)

Hammond P, Moseley M. *Trust me I'm a doctor (an insider's guide to getting the most out of the health service)*. London: Metro publishing, 1999. (For a jaundiced and, I hope, outdated view.) (ISBN 1900512602)

Your school's perspective

Dr Simon Thorn, Head of Biology, Radley College, Oxfordshire

3

It might appear odd for a teacher to be giving advice on applying to medical school but I do have a peculiar perspective on the process; I was a medical student before completing a Bachelor of Science (BSc) degree and Doctor of Philosophy (PhD) qualification in physiology. I abandoned research to become a biology teacher after an attack by animal rights activists.

This chapter will discuss how your school or college can help you in choosing a medical career.

Applicants' challenge

There is a need in this country for dedicated and able young medical students to maintain the standards of healthcare we expect. Due to the continually increasing number of applications for a limited number of places, it has been necessary for medical schools to make most selections on the basis of A level grades. The level of offers made through UCAS has risen over the past 15 years from BCC to ABB. This deters less academic but perfectly able candidates. However, it encourages more academic students to consider medicine, rather than other degrees, on the basis of status.

How can this situation be alleviated? Medical schools cannot scout for talent — they can only consider those who apply. Places are offered on the basis of academic record, references, personal statement and, more often than not, interview. In addition, some medical schools have devised their own tests to provide further data on which to select students. It is, thus, incumbent on all secondary schools to encourage their sixth-formers who are best suited to medicine to apply, and to give them the best chance of fulfilling their potential.

What should a medic be like?

At a recent UCAS seminar for medical admissions tutors across Britain, teachers and tutors were asked to summarize the qualities looked for in MEDICS. This is what was noted:

Motivation

Empathy

Dependability

Intelligence

Career-understanding

Stamina.

This rather banal mnemonic really encompasses a wide range of personal skills and attributes that medics should possess to varying degrees. As the training prepares medics for all careers within the profession, from pathology to psychiatry, a broad mix of students is essential. Nevertheless, the common elements might be exemplified as:

Motivation: a commitment, drive and ambition to achieve goals.

Empathy: a humane understanding of other people and willingness to put their comfort above your own.

Dependability: an ability to consider problems and make decisions even under pressure, both as a team member and team leader.

Intelligence: common sense and a quick grasp of concepts and factual details, with the ability to communicate effectively.

Career-understanding: an insight into the variety of skills, working conditions and stresses involved in practising medicine.

Stamina: enough physical and emotional strength to cope with the course and the career.

Role of the secondary school

The selection and preparation process begins, to a certain extent, at school. Students who show an interest in studying medicine can be encouraged and helped to make decisions that are in their best interest, eg which A levels to choose, which undergraduate courses to select and to which universities to apply. I am not going to make any recommendations here except that students and teachers inform themselves.

This section will give an indication of the school's role in:
- acquiring medical knowledge
- gaining work experience
- making the decision
- giving advice on UCAS

◎ preparing for an interview

◎ getting the grades in GCSEs and A levels.

Where to get medical knowledge

There is a panoply of resources available. A school library or careers room should stock enough up-to-date material to keep the students, teachers and parents informed. The main sources of information are listed below.

Books: Medical biography and history can enthrall, inspire or bore in equal measures. Similarly, medical textbooks can fascinate or repel would-be medics.

Pamphlets: UCAS and other publishers produce pamphlets with current advice and helpful information.

Journals: *New Scientist* gives an appropriate overview of current issues and developments in science, including biomedical topics. Recent issues of journals such as *The British Medical Journal*, *The Lancet* and *The Journal of the Royal Society of Medicine* can be obtained from a helpful doctor. These journals have editorial and news sections discussing issues with which anyone interested in medicine should be familiar.

Newspapers: The broadsheets have weekly medical and health features. Medical developments, scandals and policies are always newsworthy and cuttings can easily be assembled into a scrapbook.

Internet: The Internet can provide much interesting information but can also be a source of distraction. Choose your search keywords carefully. Surf the university websites and those of the various Royal Colleges (eg the Royal College of Surgeons and the Royal College of Physicians) and the Royal Society of Medicine and British Medical Association.

Videos: Television documentaries (eg Panorama and Horizon) and medical soaps can provide extremely good stimulus-material for group discussions on ethics. A valuable library of resources can be built up in a comparatively short time.

Prospectuses: Courses, towns and universities are all different. You should read about intake requirements, course structure and university facilities (such as accommodation and sports).

Clinical club: There will be others at your school who will want to be doctors, vets, dentists, nurses, radiographers or physiotherapists. Much can be gained by meeting together regularly to discuss matters of concern, such as ethical issues, or to give talks on your own work experiences. The club will also give you a foretaste of the camaraderie that exists at medical schools, when you will be busy studying together while others are out partying.

How to gain work experience

Before you can work in any healthcare setting you must have been vaccinated against Hepatitis B. It can be quite daunting, and often difficult, arranging clinical observation or practical work experience. Some doctors and hospitals have been criticized in the past for having mere school children in potentially dangerous and highly sensitive clinical situations. Conversely, many doctors are keen to encourage the right person to join the profession.

Your school can help by developing a network of past pupils and parents who are medics. These doctors will have a personal interest in ensuring that you get the best possible learning experience. Many will also be happy to visit your school and give talks about their clinical work or research.

Similarly, with regular contact your school can build up links with local practices and hospitals. These should not be restricted to giving help to prospective medical students. Schools can provide young people to help with voluntary work of all descriptions from serving in a friend's shop to decorating children's wards at Christmas.

How to make that final decision

This is possibly the most difficult decision you need to make and one you must make yourself. There can be immense pressures on you to become a doctor, eg there have always been doctors in your family; your parents always wanted you to be a doctor; the status of the job will be a step up the social ladder; your teachers say that, with your great academic potential, you owe it to yourself; and people keep saying what a great doctor you would make.

Remember, it is your decision and yours alone. To enable you to make that decision wisely you must explore your vocation and other academic alternatives.

Deciding on your future involves testing your willingness and commitment to helping others even when it may be unpleasant for you. You may find voluntary work with the disabled or elderly extremely challenging but also rewarding. You should talk through your experiences with a medic as well, so that you can relate them to the career that might await you.

Choosing your career is your decision, and yours alone

Exploring other academic alternatives involves finding out more about biomedical sciences. The research fields of physiology, biochemistry, anatomy, pharmacology and genetics, among many others, might provide the academic challenge you need while still satisfying your vocation to improve mankind's health and welfare.

Universities and Colleges Admission System (UCAS)

The process of applying through UCAS is, in some ways, different for you as a prospective medic. You have a very limited number of universities from which to choose — 24 in 1999 and 2000 (Table 1) — and are restricted to applying to only four. Your application must also be sent earlier than the general date (15th October in 2000). If you are thinking of taking a year out (called a gap year), consult your school's university liaison officer. If you wish to apply for deferred entry, you will need to be a very strong candidate and to have made plans for your gap year by the time of your interview. You should keep in touch with your school if you want to apply post-A level and should ensure that you will be available for interview during your year out.

Which university? What should guide your choices?

Although the quality and content of all courses must meet the criteria set by the General Medical Council (GMC), their style and flavour are all very different. You should familiarize yourself with the distinction between the 'traditional' preclinical–clinical courses and the now more widespread 'integrated' courses (discussed in another chapter). The degree of integration varies from school to school. You should also examine the balance between academic and clinical teaching; medical schools attached to hospitals

---

Table 1   The 24 medical schools (some attached to hospitals and others to universities) in the UK

London schools:
- Imperial College School of Medicine
- King's, Guy's and St Thomas' School of Medicine
- Royal Free and University College Medical School
- St Bartholomew's and the Royal London School of Medicine, Queen Mary and Westfield College
- St George's Hospital Medical School

Others:
- Aberdeen
- Birmingham
- Bristol
- Cambridge
- Dundee
- Edinburgh
- Glasgow
- Leeds
- Leicester
- Liverpool
- Manchester
- Newcastle upon Tyne
- Nottingham
- Oxford
- Queen's University of Belfast
- St Andrews
- Sheffield
- Southampton
- Wales College of Medicine

incline towards clinical research, whereas university medical schools will have close associations with biomedical faculties. For example, The University of Bristol is unique in having veterinary, medical and dental schools.

All medical schools prepare students for all branches of medicine, but it might be worth considering which hospitals are used in clinical rotations for medical students. Remember, also, that there is enormous competition for places, but the ration of applicants per places varies. UCAS publish current statistics.

Your choice of two 'insurance' non-medical courses can be to the same universities as any of your medical applications. If you do not succeed in getting into medical school first time, you can always apply to read medicine as a postgraduate after having completed a degree in another subject.

The city and university setting should also influence your choice; the course is long so you want to be happy wherever you end up. After reading official and alternative prospectuses, leafing through tourist guides and talking to friends and family, you should visit those on your shortlist. The question you need to ask yourself is, 'Do I feel at home?'.

Your personal statement

There could be as many different pieces of advice on personal statements as there are medical admissions tutors — there is no right way. The most important feature is that it should be an honest account of your interest in and commitment to becoming a doctor. If you misrepresent yourself in reference to hobbies, books, places or people with which or whom you have had little real contact, you will be found out and everything you wrote that was true will be doubted.

Remember that the personal statement is exactly what it says. There is a temptation to allow parents and teachers to rewrite it to a point where the only original thought of yours on the page is 'I want to be a doctor'. Resist this! Your character must shine through. You should, nevertheless, write grammatically and spell correctly (these are basic skills a doctor must have) and remember that your handwriting or typeface should be legible when reduced to 71% (A4 to A5) on a photocopier.

You might find it helpful to structure your personal statement in sections covering:

◎ your reasons for studying medicine
◎ how you found out about what it is like to be a doctor
◎ what you have gained from work experience
◎ your hobbies and interests within and outside school
◎ your outstanding qualities.

Your school's reference

The reference prepared by your school should be a fair assessment of your current academic and personal development. Each school will have its own format for preparing this, but it is important that the teacher(s) responsible for writing yours actually knows you. You should discuss with them your motives for becoming a doctor and the preparation you have done.

Your personal and academic strengths should be apparent and easily understood by the admissions tutors who will read the reference. One possible approach is to structure the reference as follows:

◎ general character reference

◎ individual subject references including your predicted grades in bold type

◎ an appraisal of your suitability for medicine as a course and a career.

Once you have received an offer, it's up to you to make the grades

How to prepare for interview

Most medical schools conduct interviews but each has its own style and format. Some ask for examples of your work, some require you to complete a psychometric test, and some set an admissions test. To prepare yourself for these you should:

Read the prospectus thoroughly. You will look foolish if you appear ignorant of information to be found in the prospectus. Study the course structures and content. Find out about the accommodation and student facilities.

Take advantage of open days. Your confidence and answers at an interview will reflect how well you feel at home in this relatively unfamiliar environment. Only by visiting the place and meeting the students will you be able to get a feel for it.

Practice your interview technique. Your university interviews may be the first time you will experience the pressure of being questioned by unfamiliar people. The interview may be conducted by a panel or by a couple of tutors. They will want to find out about you and your strengths. You should try to arrange practice interviews with your teachers and, if possible, a qualified doctor. The mock interviewers should have copies of your UCAS form and should give you some feedback; this will help fill in some of the gaps in your knowledge and to conquer any nerves that might prevent your best qualities from shining through. You could even try recording interviews on video and criticizing your own weaknesses in presentation.

How to get the grades — no grades, no place

GCSEs

You should have a good portfolio of high grades at GCSE or Scottish Standard Grade. These should include English, mathematics and separate or dual award sciences. Check prospectuses for individual university requirements. If you have qualifications other than GCSEs, you should contact each university admissions office for clarification.

A levels

Medical schools are revising their entry requirements in the light of Curriculum 2000. They have all welcomed the opportunity for an increase in breadth and most explicitly encourage you to take advantage of the new system and take an AS (half an A level), or even A2 (a full A level), in an arts or humanity subject. To make yourself most widely acceptable to as many medical schools as possible, you should take chemistry to A2 (although some will accept AS) and biology or biology (human) to AS. Most medical schools have recognized that students starting the course without biology at A level have a lot of catching up to do. Some also suggest that physics at AS is helpful. However, an exact combination is not prescribed; students are chosen on the basis of their personal qualities not on a magic formula of subjects. In any case, as discussed in earlier chapters, you should be predicted at least grades ABB in A level chemistry and two other subjects (except general studies). You may also have two A2 and two or more AS.

As medical schools are currently developing their policies with respect to Curriculum 2000, it is advisable to check their websites for the latest information on AS/A2 requirements, particularly with regard to retakes and resitting modules. Medical schools will not be prejudiced against applicants whose schools' policies are to 'cash in' or sit AS at the same time as A2 in year 13 (upper sixth), rather than in year 12 (lower sixth) in time to put results on the UCAS form. However, if you do have AS results, you should declare them on the form. Currently, certificated levels in Key Skills will not be accepted. If you are taking International Baccalaureate (IB) or Scottish Highers you should consult each university prospectus or website and the UCAS handbook for specific requirements.

Study skills

Once you have received an offer, it is up to you to make the grade. There may be a temptation to relax but you are barely halfway there. All universities make more offers than they have places expecting that some of you will fail to reach their requirements. This means underscoring, even by one UCAS point, could cost you your place.

Ask your teachers how you are doing. If you are not on course for an A grade or you are not doing as well as you hoped, do not give up. Ask them what you need to do to improve. It will be a pleasure for them to see you work hard and achieve your ambition.

You may need to adjust your working and social habits. You might need to develop better reading and noting skills. You will certainly have to develop appropriate examination techniques. There are many revision and study guides available. Look at a few recommended ones and choose one that you like. You must be diligent about putting its advice into practice.

Figure 1 summarizes the basic stages and steps involved in obtaining a place at medical school.

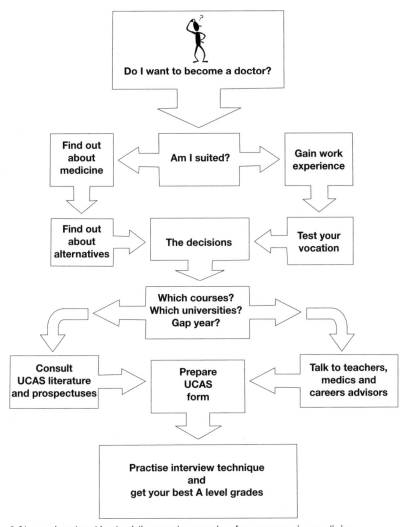

Figure 1 Stages involved in deciding and preparing for a career in medicine

Further reading

The big guide. University and college entrance: the official guide 2001 (UCAS). UCAS, 2000. (ISBN 0948241802)

A student's guide to entry to medicine (UCAS). UCAS, 2000.

Corps L, Urmston I. *The insiders guide to medical schools (the alternative prospectus)* 1999. London: *BMJ* Publishing Group, 1999. (ISBN 0727914286)

British Medical Association. *Medical careers — a general guide*. London: *BMJ* Publishing Group, 1994. (ISBN 0727910876)

The interview

Professor John Stein, Medical Tutor, Magdalen College, Oxford University

4

Most medical schools interview all applicants whom they feel have a reasonable chance of getting a place. This means that about one-third of applicants are invited for interview. The medical schools attached to the Universities of St Andrew's and Edinburgh and the Queen's University of Belfast currently (1999) do not interview those who have not yet taken their A levels, often called pre-A level candidates.

Purpose of the interview

There are two main aims of the interview:

◎   to judge your enthusiasm, commitment and suitability for medicine

◎   to assess your academic potential.

The second point is not as important for universities that focus less on the basic sciences behind medicine — such universities are satisfied with the evidence provided by your school report and your GCSE and A level performances.

> ❝ Dress smartly, do not be late, and read the prospectus beforehand ❞

Useful hints

There are a few general rules to remember.

- ◎ You are trying to communicate your commitment and enthusiasm for medicine, so do not give the impression of being unsure, shifty and possibly dishonest by looking away from your interviewers all the time. Look them straight in the eye as much as possible, and smile frequently to show that you are really confident of your vocation.

- ◎ You are trying to persuade this particular set of selectors to offer you a place at their medical school, so make the effort to find out what is special about their medical course and institution — it may be the history, the buildings, the town in which it is located, the research excellence or the integrated course.

- ◎ The public expect their doctors to be people they can admire and rely on. Mainly they hope to trust your knowledge and experience of disease, but outward and visible symbols are also important. Therefore, even though your peers might think it 'uncool' to wear a suit and tie, you should dress smartly for your interview, you must not be late, and you should prepare for it by at the very least having read the prospectus and knowing what that particular medical school has to offer.

- ◎ To assess your commitment, the interviewers will definitely ask you, in one form or another, why you want to study medicine. There is no perfect answer to this question, but you should use it as an opportunity to explain your particular interests in medicine and your actions for acquainting yourself with what it is really like through your work experience, voluntary service in a hospital, hospice, old people's home or clinic, nursing, hospital portering or service of other kinds.

- ◎ Your interviewers will also probably be interested in your views on current medical issues, such as the funding of the National Health Service, ensuring the quality of doctors' performance (now known as clinical governance), euthanasia, or the pros and cons of the new genetics. You need to have some knowledge on these issues and to have formed your own opinions on them. There are no correct answers, but your remarks will help the interviewers to judge how much you have bothered to think about burning political and ethical issues in UK medicine.

- ◎ Selectors will be trying to assess your general enthusiasm, intelligence, energy, interpersonal skills and self-organization. Thus, they will probably ask you about your other interests, eg academic, cultural or sporting. This is not because there is anything intrinsically 'better' about being a county chess player over playing football for your school, but because its shows that you have wider interests and that you can organize your time well enough to achieve a high standard academically and also pursue your other interests to a similarly high standard.

◎ The second purpose of the interview that is especially important for schools concentrating on the basic sciences behind medicine (eg the Universities of Oxford and Cambridge) is for the interviewers to try to make a finer judgement about your academic ability and potential than GCSE and A level predictions provide. Thus, they will probably ask you about an aspect of your A level course that you have found particularly interesting. Ritual humiliation at interview is a thing of the past. Nowadays, we are not trying to expose what you do not know. We want to find out what you do know and then assess: how you use that knowledge to support an argument; how deeply you have delved into the subject to find out how it really works; how well you can think on your feet; and how clearly and logically you can express the results of your thought processes. You will often be given a problem to solve there and then, or be taught something new to see how you cope with it. Take it slowly and do not be afraid to admit if you think you have made a mistake. One of the most important lessons any doctor has to learn is how to recognize when they are wrong.

Summary

◎ Make sure you have some knowledge about the special features of that particular medical school.

◎ Be prepared to talk about current socio-medical and medico-political issues, such as euthanasia or financing the health service.

◎ If you are applying for a course that emphasizes the basic sciences, be prepared to talk in some detail about why you are interested in them and how they relate to medicine.

◎ Above all, communicate your commitment, enthusiasm and energy.

How to choose a medical school

5

Professor David Lowe & Nick Loman, St Bartholomew's and the Royal London
School of Medicine and Dentistry, London

There are now only four spaces on the UCAS form for medical school applications. Before you contemplate the relative merits of clubbing in Liverpool or London, or shopping in Edinburgh or Glasgow, you must first consider whether or not you satisfy the entrance requirements. Medical schools receive thousands of application forms each year that will eventually be thrown away as the applicant did not read the prospectus details correctly. You may regard this as a remarkable injustice, but no matter how perfectly crafted your personal statement and how complimentary your reference, your application will go no further if you do not have a suitable A level selection and the required GCSE grades for your chosen medical school.

Medical school admission is a precise, almost military-style operation — it has to be! Application forms are received over a period of several months, when busy consultants and lecturers give up their time to read them and the admissions staff will be stretched to their limits processing them. The thousands of keen hopefuls must somehow be whittled down to a mere handful of hundreds for interview.

If you are a retake candidate, you should check the prospectus carefully as some medical schools will not accept such students.

Examples of exceptional entrance requirements

- St George's Hospital Medical School asks for six A or A⁺ grades at GCSE
- The Universities of Oxford and Cambridge expect three predicted A grades at A level
- All medical schools ask for A level chemistry, but not all require a second science subject

---

Things to check:

- ◎ Do my GCSE grades satisfy the entrance requirements?
- ◎ Are my A level subjects suitable?
- ◎ Does this medical school accept retake candidates?

Several factors (eg type of institution, approach to examinations and location) should be considered to help you with your choice of school; some of these are discussed below.

Will the course provide advantages when applying for jobs?

All medical school teaching is taught according to the standards set out by the GMC. You can be sure that any medical school you attend will provide you with a standard of education good enough to ensure you will be able to practise medicine at the end. It is generally regarded as an advantage to go to a London medical school if you want to work in London after you qualify; the same is true for other regional schools. If, for example, you have a particular interest in research science, you may want to study at the high-flying academic institutions such as Oxbridge or Imperial College.

Examination procedure – slow and steady, or a race for the finish?

Examinations are changing at medical school. Traditionally, the approach has been high-intensity, zero sleep marathon revision sessions for the dreaded

'end of years'. This approach is slowly being phased out in most medical schools. 'Continuous assessment' is the new buzz word which means a greater frequency of examination assessments but in smaller, more manageable chunks. The Universities of Oxford and Cambridge, however, remain an exception to this trend and have a very intensive (but mercifully short) term structure.

Do I feel confident about interviews?

Your skills in communication will be very important as a doctor, but if you feel the pressure to succeed at your medical school interview will turn you into a gibbering wreck, it may be helpful to note that not all medical schools interview. The Universities of Southampton and St Andrew's, for example, only interview mature and overseas applicants, and the University of Edinburgh and the Queen's University, Belfast only interview a small number of pre-A level applicants. Conversely, if you feel your personal skills will outshine your application form, then you may want to apply to universities that interview as many applicants as possible, for example University of Leicester which aims to interview 50% of its applicants.

What is the area like?

Spare some consideration for your feelings about where you live. If you support a football team 300 miles away from your home town, this might be your opportunity to get a bit closer. If you are from a small village in Orkney, you may want to sample the excitement and buzz of London for the first time — or the idea might terrify you.

For the pre-clinical phase, most medical schools are based in large cities and should give you enough to do. However, in the clinical phase, the large number of medical students means that you will be spread out across the hospitals in the area. At St Bartholomew's and the Royal London School of Medicine, Queen Mary and Westfield College, London, you may find yourself not just at the Royal Hospitals, but as far away as Southend-on-Sea. Cambridge students do much learning at the Norfolk and Norwich hospitals. This provides the opportunity to sample a variety of communities but can leave you wondering what you are doing there, and missing your friends.

If you are from the coast, you may find moving to a medical school without easy access to the sea distressing, in which case, you should not apply to Leicester. If you are a lover of dramatic scenery and surroundings, Scotland may be the place for you.

Do I want to go to medical school or university?

Most provincial medical schools have always been part of a university. Some have only recently merged with universities, mainly those in London. Only one, St George's, remains independent of a larger institution.

In London, Guy's, King's and St Thomas', formed from the merger of King's College London and UMDS (formerly Guy's and St Thomas'), is such a recent merger that the effects are still being felt. St Bartholomew's and the

Royal London Hospital have been merged with Queen Mary and Westfield (QMW) for a number of years, and integration is slowly becoming a reality for new pre-clinical students. At Sheffield, much emphasis is placed on mixing between medical students and the rest of the university. This certainly opens you up to a range of new experiences, but you may find that the course becomes harder if you try and keep up with the lifestyles of other students.

What style of course is running?

Most medical schools have introduced 'integrated' curricula where the old distinctions between 'pre-clinical' (mainly book learning) and 'clinical' (working in the hospital) have faded. Teaching is no longer based on a course of anatomy, pharmacology and physiology but is now 'systems-based', usually for the first two years with significant emphasis on 'problem-based learning' and the last three years being clinically based. However, some schools such as Aberdeen have eroded this clinical/pre-clinical distinction completely. The Universities of Oxford and Cambridge remain very traditional with a science-based course including a project element for the first three years, following onto the clinical phase either locally or at a London school.

Do I want to do an intercalated BSc? Would I like the choice?

Some courses have changed to six years and force you to take an intercalated BSc degree (studying the final year of a 'conventional' degree) at that university, eg Imperial. Most London medical schools have good provision for going to do a BSc at either the end of the second year or as a clinical BSc after the fourth year, and often you can study at the same university or at another London college. At other colleges, BSc degrees are restricted to those with a proven certain level of academic proficiency.

Is variety the spice of life?

The Universities of Oxford and Cambridge will allow you to continue your clinical studies in London or at the 'other' college. London will give you the option to apply onto the Oxbridge course if accompanied by a BSc.

Am I taking a pre-medical course?

For those with good non-science A levels, or graduates with non-science degrees, some schools offer a pre-medical course which lasts an additional

Table 1 Medical schools that offer a pre-medical course	
• Bristol	• Manchester
• Dundee	• Newcastle upon Tyne
• Edinburgh	• Sheffield
• Guy's, King's and St Thomas' School of Medicine	• Wales College of Medicine

year (Table 1). The entrance requirements are usually slightly higher than those of the shorter course, and places are limited. If you are applying for such a course your choices will be limited.

Financial issues

Conventional wisdom assumes that living in London is more expensive than anywhere else. By the same token, the north of England is regarded as 'cheap'. This is not necessarily true. Students studying at St Bartholomew's and the Royal London School of Medicine can find accommodation as cheap as £40/week if they live further out of the city centre. On the other hand, a one bedroom flat near St Bartholomew's Hospital starts at about £200/week. In fact, some universities have such a large student population (eg Cambridge, Oxford and Bristol) that cheap accommodation is hard to come by.

Further reading

Corps L, Urmston I. *The insiders guide to medical schools (the alternative prospectus) 1999*. London: BMJ Publishing Group, 1999. (ISBN 0727914286)

Website http://www.mds.qmw.ac.uk/admissions. St Bartholomew's and the Royal London School of Medicine and Dentistry operate a discussion forum for prospective students to talk about the admissions process, swap hints about work experience, and offer support and advice on this website.

Career pathways in medicine

Dr Elisabeth Paice, Dean Director of Postgraduate Medical & Dental Education, North Thames

6

After graduating and leaving medical school, you will enter the postgraduate training system where you will need to make career choices that will influence the rest of your life in medicine.

Postgraduate training follows two major pathways:

◎ towards becoming a principal in general practice (primary care)

◎ towards becoming a consultant in a specialty.

Training takes place within three grades: pre-registration house officer (PRHO), senior house officer (SHO) and registrar. Clinical academic training follows the same broad pattern, but allows time out for research or concurrent research and clinical training (Figure 1). Postgraduate training is

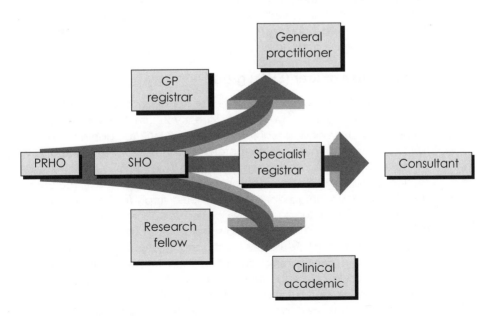

Figure 1   Career pathways in medicine

managed by the regional postgraduate dean, to standards and curricula determined by the Royal Colleges. Registration as a medical practitioner, GP or specialist is a matter for the GMC.

Postgraduate training system

Pre-registration house officer (PRHO) grade

Once you have passed finals, you will be a doctor but not yet a registered medical practitioner. First you have to demonstrate that you can put your training into practice. The PRHO year gives you the opportunity to do this under close supervision. PRHO posts (called 'house jobs') may consist of six months of medicine and six months of surgery, or four months each of medicine, surgery and another specialty like general practice (primary care), paediatrics or psychiatry. Your medical school will probably have a matching scheme to help you find a house job. The specialties undertaken as a PRHO do not need to be related to your career intentions. A house job with exposure to general practice (primary care), for example, may be particularly useful for those intending a career in hospital medicine who may never have another chance to experience work in the community. House jobs in teaching hospitals may be highly sought after, but often district general hospitals offer broader experience, a friendlier atmosphere and better supervision. The important thing is to choose an environment in which you feel comfortable and a consultant with whom you get on — the PRHO year is stressful enough without adding interpersonal conflict. If your medical school is a long way from home, you may want to get a house job nearer your friends and family.

Senior house officer (SHO) grade

After the PRHO year, provided your performance is considered satisfactory as it will be in more than 95% of cases, you are 'signed up' by your consultant supervisor and registered with the GMC. You can now move on to the SHO grade. There are no matching schemes for this grade and you will have to obtain a position, eg by looking in medical journals' Classified section for advertisements, and apply in open competition. If you are sure about what you want to do, then you should apply for SHO posts that will take you towards your goal. Those aiming for general practice (primary care) can join a vocational training scheme that currently consists of four hospital SHO posts of six months each, and a year as a GP registrar in a practice. Those aiming for a consultant post in one of the 60 or more specialties should check the entry criteria for the specialty of their choice, which will usually set out the experience required at SHO level and any examinations that need to have been passed. Most specialties or groups of specialties have SHO rotations that deliver the experience and provide tuition toward the examinations. A general surgical or general medical rotation will prepare you for a group of surgical or medical specialties. Some posts at this level are suitable for starting out in a range of specialties and give you the opportunity to gain useful experience while you are deciding or trying to enter the more competitive fields. Accident and emergency medicine is an example. Most doctors spend two to three years at the SHO grade. Changing specialty, taking time out to go abroad or for research, failing examinations or repeated attempts to enter an oversubscribed specialty will all lengthen the time spent at this level.

Specialist registrar programmes

Higher specialist training is now delivered through one specialist registrar grade, which replaces the previous two grades of registrar and senior registrar. Entry to a specialist registrar training programme is by open competition, but you must meet the entry criteria (specified SHO experience and examinations in most cases). Specialties differ in their competitiveness, and for the more popular ones you will have to convince an appointments panel of your superiority in terms of aptitude and commitment. Once you have been appointed to a specialist registrar programme, you are given a national training number (NTN). This is the passport that allows you to stay in the programme, rotating within a group of teaching and district general hospitals and having annual assessments (and possibly more examinations) until you have completed a defined curriculum. At the end of three to six years, depending on the specialty, you receive a certificate of completion of specialist training (accreditation on the specialist register) and are eligible to take up a consultant post.

Research and academic training

All doctors need to understand the principles of research, if only to be able to read research papers in journals with a critical eye. Some doctors will wish to have a more active research involvement and will become clinical academics, ie professors leading a research unit as well as undertaking the care of patients. Opportunities for research start in medical school. Most schools offer, and some insist on, one year out of medicine to do an intercalated Bachelor of Arts (BA) or BSc degree that will usually involve a research project. Your success in this will be taken as a pointer to your research potential if you wish to pursue research later. There is also the possibility of taking time out to study for and obtain a higher degree (eg PhD, Doctor of Medicine (MD) or Master of Surgery (MS)) during medical school. Once you have qualified, it is aswell to get a few years experience under your belt before taking time out for serious research. You will wish to decide on a specialty and demonstrate your aptitude for it, and then consider how research will dovetail with your clinical career. Most research will require you to obtain grants in open competition for a well thought-out

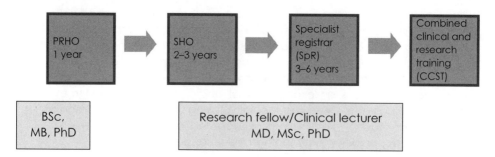

Figure 2   Steps in training for clinical research

project, so you will need good advice from someone senior and successful in the research field that interests you. You will need to work towards a research degree, usually a PhD (three years), MD (two years) or Master of Science (MSc) (at least one year). The clinical lecturer grade offers the opportunity to combine clinical and research training (Figure 2).

Choice of specialty

Most people starting medical school would be prepared to consider a wide range of careers within medicine, just as long as they were a doctor. Some have a very clear career aim. Most surgeons you talk to will say they always knew they wanted to do surgery, although a good proportion of those who think they want to do surgery at the start later change their minds. Psychiatry and general practice (primary care) are specialties that people often turn to later, especially if they get fed up with hospital life. In general, the more you are exposed to a specialty in medical school, the more likely you are to choose it as a career. For this reason, more medical schools are organizing undergraduate training in general practice (primary care), where the numbers of doctors entering is less than needed to maintain the service. Figure 3 shows the career intentions of a group of PRHOs. At present, 40% of doctors work in general practice (primary care), but only 20% of PRHOs intend to enter this field as a career. Most people will change their minds several times during the course of medical school, the PRHO year and, to a lesser extent, subsequently. Once you have reached the registrar grade, it is much more difficult to change specialty or move between hospital and general practice (primary care).

The major specialties are listed in Table 1. More important than which diseases or which system you wish to concentrate on are questions about your style of working and preferred environment. You need to consider whether you prefer working closely with others in a team, or working

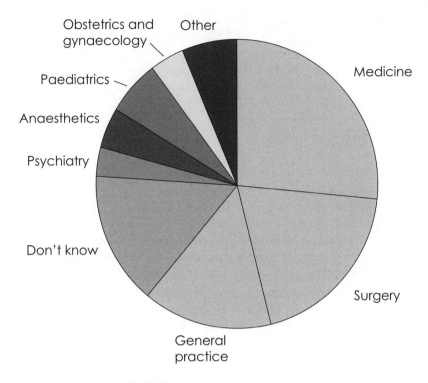

Figure 3   Career intentions of PRHOs

independently without having to consult or communicate with others. In general, medicine offers fewer opportunities for the latter, as the single-handed GP is being replaced by group practices and the hospital consultant is now part of a clinical directorate. You should consider whether or not you like to work in a hospital or would prefer being out in the community, as a GP, a community paediatrician or perhaps a public health doctor. Are you more interested in talking with patients or in carrying out procedures? Do you prefer the world of wards and clinics, the atmosphere of the operating theatre or the relative quietness of the laboratory? Does 'high tech' equipment turn you on or terrify you? Are you easily bored or easily stressed?

As you progress through medical school you will have the opportunity to observe doctors working in a variety of environments. Talk to them about their specialty in the light of the factors listed above, and ask them what qualities are needed to succeed in their field. The happiest doctors are those whose jobs best fit their characters. Virtually all doctors will need

Table 1 Major medical specialties	
• Accident and emergency	• Paediatrics
• Anaesthetics	• Pathology
• General practice (primary care)	• Psychiatry
• Medicine	• Public health
• Obstetrics and gynaecology	• Radiology
• Occupational medicine	• Surgery
• Ophthalmology	

commitment, intelligence (including 'emotional intelligence'), self control, integrity and an interest in people. Sixth-formers wondering about a career in medicine often ask, 'What if I can't stand the sight of blood?' That problem, in fact, passes rapidly. What is much more important is being able to stand the sight of people — coping with sick, confused, demanding patients and their anxious, perhaps angry, relatives.

What about having a life? It is hard to achieve a good balance between home and work anywhere in medicine, but some specialties are more 'family friendly' than others as they have fewer emergencies. If you have children, or have some other well-founded reason for not being able to continue full-time training, there are opportunities for training less than full-time. Every year, more than one-half of medical graduates are women, and opportunities for flexible (part-time) training are much more accessible than used to be the case. It should be possible to arrange flexible training at any grade and in every specialty, anywhere in the UK. In each region there will be a person in charge of administering the scheme, usually an associate postgraduate dean, who will be able to give you more details. Each Royal College also has somebody who will give advice about flexible training in their specialty. While specialties with little emergency work, such as dermatology or public health medicine, have obvious appeal for doctors with young families, many women work part-time within busy specialties like paediatrics or anaesthetics, planning child-care arrangements well ahead so they can take their turn in on-call rotas.

Role of the postgraduate dean

Each region has a postgraduate dean who is responsible for managing postgraduate medical education and training. The postgraduate dean commissions the hospital or practice to train a given number of doctors in agreed specialties and grades; the dean also puts funds into a postgraduate education centre in each hospital, with a library, centre manager, GP vocational training scheme course organizer and clinical tutor. The clinical tutor or centre manager will have information about careers, including the entry requirements for each specialty. The postgraduate dean is responsible for monitoring the quality of training in each post, and will probably visit each hospital once every year or two to interview trainees. The deanery manages recruitment to the specialist registrar grade, awards NTNs and carries out a range of administrative tasks associated with the management of training programmes. Every deanery has a specialty training committee for each specialty, where representatives of the Royal College, postgraduate dean and consultant trainers meet to organize the training. There are also likely to be associate deans for flexible training, overseas doctors, PRHOs or counselling, depending on the size and structure of the deanery. Directors of Postgraduate GP Education manage the training of intended GPs.

First experience of your medical career

Unless you come from a medical family or have had a lot to do with medicine, the first experience of working as a doctor can be quite a shock. There are some really tough transitions to cope with. As a final-year student, you are responsible only for yourself, you can decide when to go to sleep and when to get up, when to study and when to relax — you are at the top of the medical student hierarchy. As a new house officer, you are at the bottom of the medical hierarchy, you have jobs that must be done, no matter how tired or hungry you are, everyone seems to know more than you and seems to be authorized to order you about. In addition, you have to cope with being very close to the human tragedies of disease and death.

Most house officers question their decision to become a doctor during this first year. They find the intensity and hours of work very hard, especially if much of the work is mundane and does not seem to require the medical training they have received. They resent the impact of the hours and their tiredness on their social lives. They look at the lifestyle of friends who have gone into 'boring' jobs, such as banking or accountancy, with some envy. The pay, while welcome, does not seem commensurate with the hours of work. Some find the burden of responsibility for others hard to bear.

On the brighter side, very few house officers drop out. Less than 1% decide medicine is not for them and leave their jobs in that first year, which is undoubtedly the hardest and most stressful year of a medical career. There are also rewards. House officers have said the things they enjoyed about being a doctor were the teamwork, the contact with people, the challenge and variety of work, the privilege of being part of people's lives at crucial times and, most importantly, the sense of making a difference. That is what doctors go into medicine for and what sustains them through the long training, the hard work and the emotional demands of the profession.

Ethical issues in modern medical practice

7

Professor Raanan Gillon, Emeritus Professor of Medical Ethics, Imperial College of Science, Technology and Medicine, London

This chapter will give an insight into ethical issues in modern medical practice, and will focus on how these issues can be approached.

Medical ethics

One of the skills you will need these days if you become a doctor is some knowledge of medical ethics and medical law, and an ability to think reasonably and critically about medical ethics issues in general. The GMC, which controls medical education and medical standards in the UK, has specified that medical ethics and law should be part of the core curriculum for medical students[1]. A couple of years ago, most medical school teachers of these subjects drew up a core curriculum outlining subjects that students should study during medical school[2]. So, as a medical student, you will have to come to know the main professional and legal obligations of doctors in the UK and to get to grips with the following ethically and legally important subjects:

◎ Informed consent and refusal of treatment.

◎ Truthfulness, trust and good communications in the doctor–patient relationship.

◎ Confidentiality and privacy.

◎ Medical research, its connections with ordinary therapeutic medical practice, and the special ethical and legal concerns relevant to it.

◎ A variety of ethical and legal aspects of human reproduction, eg those associated with embryo research, in vitro fertilization and abortion.

◎ The 'new genetics', eg gene therapy, genetic testing and different forms of cloning.

◎ Treatment of children and issues such as children's rights, the relationship between age and competence to accept or refuse treatment, child abuse, and questions about decision-making on behalf of children.

- Mental illness and disorder and its associated ethical and legal problems, eg compulsory treatment of some severely mentally disordered patients.

- Life and death issues, including debates about differences between allowing patients to die and killing them, euthanasia, what is meant by 'death' and 'brain death', and doctors' legal obligations in relation to death (a relatively mundane but in practice very important example is their legal duty to certify deaths).

- Resource allocation issues and questions of distributive justice: how might we fairly distribute scarce healthcare resources? How might we fairly 'ration' such resources? What are the pros and cons of different approaches, including those of different healthcare systems, to these questions?

- Rights, including human rights — what are they and what is their role in medical ethics and law?

- The vulnerabilities that the duties of doctors and medical students, and the public expectations of them, create. Various issues that can have adverse effects on doctors and medical students also need ethical and legal exploration, eg the need to be able to deal with uncertainty, various legal and professional regulations that apply to doctors, public expectations and concerns, ill health afflicting doctors and medical students themselves, and 'whistle blowing' when a medical student or doctor believes something unethical and/or illegal is going on around him or her.

This is quite an extensive list of ethical and legal issues to think about over the few years of medical studies, not to mention over the course of your professional life if you become a doctor. For my own part as a doctor who studied philosophy in order to try and think more clearly about my ethical obligations, I have found the 'four principles plus scope' approach very helpful for ordering my thoughts and summarizing my medical ethical obligations.

'Four principles plus scope' approach

The four principles are: respect for autonomy, beneficence, non-maleficence and justice. The scope of applying such principles is also an important issue: to whom or to what do we owe these obligations? These principles do not provide a method of choosing the correct one when they conflict — they are *prima facie* and do not provide a set of ordered rules or an algorithm for moral judgements. However, they do provide a common set of moral commitments, a common moral language and a common set of moral issues that can be used to help us reflect about the many ethical problems posed by medical practice.

Respect for autonomy

Autonomy can be thought of as 'deliberated self rule'. Respect for autonomy is the moral obligation to respect the autonomy of a person in so far as such respect is compatible with equal respect for the autonomy of all potentially affected. In modern medical practice, this principle has many *prima facie* implications. It requires doctors to consult patients and give them adequate information and obtain their consent before the patient can be helped and treated. It also requires doctors not to deceive patients, eg not to deceive them about the diagnosis of their illness unless, of course, they do not wish to be told.

This principle even means that doctors, and other healthcare professionals, should be punctual for their appointments — an agreed appointment with a patient is a type of promise, and arriving late or not keeping the appointment would be breaking the promise and, thus, not respecting the patient's autonomy.

Medical confidentiality is another example of respecting the patient's autonomy. Patients tell doctors their symptoms, worries and other personal information in confidence, and doctors promise to keep these 'secrets' to themselves. Such promises of confidentiality are important not only because they respect patient autonomy, but also because they increase the chance of the patient obtaining the correct treatment — without these promises, patients are less likely to divulge sensitive and private information needed for optimal care. However, they are not absolute — again *prima facie*. If a patient in a confidential consultation says he or she is going to murder someone, and it is clear that they mean it, the promise is morally over-ridden by the obligation to save someone's life.

These are only a few examples of the commitment and issues related to respect for the patient's autonomy in medical practice. For these to be carried out, doctors need to have good interpersonal skills and be good communicators. They should be good listeners and should be able to give the patient relevant information when they think appropriate (eg, a run-through of treatment strategies currently available for their specific illness, suggesting the best, most suitable treatment option, and determining whether or not the patient would be interested in that particular option), as many patients choose to be involved in 'having a say' in and deciding their medical care. Others, however, do not want much information and prefer to leave the decision on their treatment to the doctor. Thus, doctors should try to ascertain the patient's needs and preferences so they can respect their autonomy.

Beneficence and non-maleficence

Beneficence means the act of doing good, and maleficence means doing harm. The traditional moral obligation in medicine, from Hippocratic times, is to provide optimal medical benefit to the patient with the least amount of harm, ie beneficence with non-maleficence. For this to be achieved, doctors should make sure that they can actually provide the benefits that they profess they can provide. They need to ensure that they have an effective education and training not only before but throughout their medical careers.

In order to offer every patient net benefit with minimal harm, the patient's own views should, where possible, be ascertained, as what may be a benefit to one patient may be harmful to another. Medical professionals should also be aware of any risks related to proposed healthcare interventions, and should really define at the outset who is likely to benefit from such interventions. This is particularly important in medical research, so as to avoid imposing risks greater than minimal on research subjects unless such risks are in the patient's own interests.

One moral concept that has become increasingly popular over the past few years is helping patients to be more in control of and take an interest in their own health. This concept is known as 'empowerment'. It is a mixture of respecting, by enhancing, patient's autonomy and beneficence, in the sense of helping them to understand how they can improve their own health.

Justice

Justice can briefly be defined as the moral obligation to act on the basis of fair adjudication between competing claims. When considering justice in medicine, there are three aspects of particular importance:

- ◎ distributive justice — fair distribution of scarce resources
- ◎ rights-based justice — respect for people's rights (including their human rights)
- ◎ legal justice — respect for morally acceptable laws.

Justice is not only about treating people equally. As Aristotle pointed out more than 2,000 years ago, it is about treating equally those who ought to be treated equally and treating unequally those who ought to be treated unequally, and doing so in proportion to the morally relevant inequalities. For example, we should all be treated equally under the law; however, the law should treat us unequally (differently) if we deserve to be treated unequally. For instance, those guilty of an offence should be treated differently from those who have not committed an offence — that is part of legal justice.

In distributing scarce healthcare resources, we should treat people unequally in relation to morally relevant inequalities. For an obvious example, people with unequal healthcare needs should be treated unequally, with more resources going to those with greater needs. There are other potentially relevant criteria as well as need, eg the amount of benefit a unit of resource will provide for both an individual patient and for a population as a whole, the views of the persons in need (they may reject what they need), and the views of the people who provide the resources (eg tax payers and their parliamentary representatives). We simply have not agreed on how to balance these conflicting moral values in a substantive theory of distributive justice (and we probably never will!). What we can, and I believe we should, do is avoid obviously unjust ways of distributing scarce resources, eg mere personal preference such as 'I like 'x' better than 'y'' or racial, social or gender prejudice, and work within democratically established procedures for balancing or 'harmonizing' conflicting moral values. We should also be open about what those procedures are, and accept that it is inevitable that there will never be enough resources to enable all the moral values to be honoured all the time, or even to enable all needs to be met. So, even if allocation is entirely fair or just, it will inevitably be resented for not meeting all needs, not honouring all conflicting moral concerns at once.

Scope of applying the principles

Many important questions arise when the scope of applying the four principles is considered. For example, to whom do healthcare professionals have a duty of beneficence? To what extent should they be helped? Who or what falls into the scope of distributing resources fairly according to the principle of justice — only the people in a particular country or internationally?

As far as beneficence is concerned, doctors clearly owe this to all their patients. But what about people who are not patients yet are ill?

Who is to be included within the scope of the principle of respect of autonomy? Some patients are clearly not included within the scope of this principle because they are not autonomous at all. For example, newborn babies are not autonomous as they are not able to deliberate. What about infants and young children, severely mentally ill people or the elderly with dementia? Will they be autonomous enough to make certain decisions, eg to have an operation? They may not be, but yet they may be able to decide what clothes to wear, which television programme they want to watch and which foods they want to eat. If such inadequately autonomous patients make decisions that seem, according to the doctor, to be against their interests, then issues such as who should make decisions on their behalf arise.

Another important scope issue is who and what has the 'right to life'? This issue remains highly controversial among healthcare professionals and in society generally. What is the right of life — the right to be kept alive or not to be unfairly killed? Who exactly has the right to life? Do non-humans (eg animals and plants) have this right? What about human embryos, foetuses and brain dead patients — are they 'people' and do they have the right to life? People often think that disagreement about such issues demonstrates radical disagreement about moral values; however, it seems to me that the disagreement is instead metaphysical (concerning the nature of reality) and/or theological, although of course it has major moral consequences. Thus, we all agree that we should not murder each other. However, we may disagree profoundly about what we mean by 'each other' and, in particular, about whether or not an embryo or a foetus (or a brain dead human being) falls within the scope of this obligation not to murder each other.

Conclusion

The 'four principles plus scope approach' provides a simple and accessible method for thinking about ethical issues in healthcare. It allows doctors from completely different moral cultures to share a common moral commitment, a common moral language and a common analytical framework for reflecting on issues that arise at work. This approach can be shared by everyone, regardless of their background, as it is culturally, philosophically and politically neutral.

References and further reading

1. General Medical Council. *Tomorrow's doctors*. London: GMC 1993: 14, 26.

2. Teachers of medical ethics and law in UK medical schools. Teaching medical ethics and law within medical education: a model for the UK core curriculum. *J Med Ethics* 1998; **24**: 188–92.

Gillon R. *Philosophical medical ethics*. London: John Wiley & Sons, 1986. (ISBN 0471912220)

Gillon R. Medical ethics: four principles plus attention to scope. *BMJ* 1994; **309**: 184–8.

Doyal L, Gillon R. Medical ethics and law as a core subject in medical education. A core curriculum offers flexibility in how it is taught — but not that it is taught. *BMJ* 1998; **316**: 1623–4.

Medical student years and how to survive them

Dr Marcus Wagstaff, Senior House Officer, Queen's Medical Centre, Nottingham

8

The previous chapters in this book have discussed choosing a medical school, the interview and how to increase your chances of obtaining a place — but what happens when you get there? What is it like? What will be expected of you? Millions of students have successfully navigated the medical course without having these questions answered before entering. This chapter aims to address the kind of queries I had before waving Mum and Dad goodbye, spinning on my heels and sprinting up the steps of University College London to a new life of seemingly carefree abandon. Issues such as finances, accommodation and welfare have not been discussed as these can be researched from any student guide, bank manager (approach with caution!) or prospectus. This chapter is purely a guide for living life as a medical student.

Two quick rules to bear in mind:

◎ Admissions tutors are an experienced and wily bunch. It is not in their best interests to offer places to students who are not capable of passing finals. So if you get an offer, they are pretty sure you can make it to becoming a doctor.

◎ If you are a school-leaver, five years is a big chunk of your youth. You would hate to look back

Apply for the medical course that best suits you as a person

on your time at medical school and think, 'Well, I was successful, but I did not get out much'. What a waste! There are so many opportunities at university to make use of your free time, you would be insane not to take them.

Course and workload

Although you have got your A levels, you are about to undergo the humiliating metamorphosis of superbrain to amoeba; but everyone else will too, so welcome to the bottom rung of a new ladder!

Courses vary and you should be familiar with the different types and what each medical school offers before applying. This will avoid you being 'taken to the cleaners' at interview regarding your inconsistency of choice.

Every medical school will tell you at length that theirs is the best course and how they differ from the others (eg more radical, free-thinking and problem-based learning study). However, there are essentially three approaches to medical training evolving from traditional, through modular, to integrated. There are professors of medical education around the country who get very excited burning the midnight oil tweaking aspects of their course. Nevertheless, all courses have to reach a standard set and evaluated by the GMC and your medical degree, no matter where you studied, is equivalent to one awarded anywhere else. Therefore, the key is to apply for courses that best suit you as a person.

Traditional approach

The traditional format, still used for example by Oxbridge, encompasses a lecture and practical-led programme in the basic medical sciences over the first two years; this is followed by clinical training on the wards in the subsequent three years. I chose this programme as I wanted to have grounding in the disciplines before being released on the unsuspecting patient without the benefits of a further two years' maturity. The sciences are separated into their constituent parts, ie anatomy, physiology, biochemistry, pathology etc (I counted 18!), on which you are formally examined at the end of each year. The structure lends itself to progression into a science-based intercalated BSc degree in the third or fourth year (discussed opposite). It may seem dry at face value, and much of it might appear irrelevant during your study, but you would be surprised just how much instant recollection of these subjects is needed throughout the clinical course and your future practice.

Modular approach

The modular format, or horizontal integration, is similar to the traditional approach except that the basic sciences are coordinated into systems, eg you may spend a month covering the structure and function of the cardiovascular system, then the gastrointestinal system and so on.

Integrated approach

The integrated, or vertical integration, course combines the clinical and pre-clinical courses for a seamless progression from student to doctor. This has the advantage of presenting the relevance of the sciences to clinical practice, which can fuel the enthusiasm so commonly lost in the pure science pre-clinical years. It also confronts the students much earlier in their course with issues such as medical ethics, doctor–patient communication and the medico-legal aspects of practice. The GMC is now recommending that all courses cover these issues from the first year (vertical spine teaching).

Intercalated BSc

It may seem a little early to be thinking about this, but it can affect your choice of medical school. More students every year take a year out from medicine in their third or fourth year to attain an extra degree. The BSc or Medical Science (BMedSci) is compulsory in some medical schools (eg University of Nottingham and Imperial College) and optional in others, with the number of places and range of courses varying greatly from school to school.

You basically spend your time studying the final year of a 'conventional' degree, of which most students choose a science or clinical subject eg anatomy, physiology, psychology or orthopaedics. Some medical schools (eg University College London), offer more diverse subjects such as the history of medicine; I remember one student in my year pursuing religious studies. Your previous years at university count and you are, therefore, awarded a full degree at the end of the year.

So, why do a BSc? Well, it presents the opportunity to study and understand a subject in more detail than the pressures of the pre-clinical course will permit. It requires you to develop a different type of thinking and learning. The work is more self-motivated and research-based often including projects in working departments rather than the 'practicals' you will be used to. Some students simply enjoy spending a year away from medicine, doing something different, and enjoying the lower time commitments that 'conventional' degrees demand (the choice between Richard and Judy and Teletubbies can be torture, if you are up in time!).

Taking the initiative and doing a BSc says something about you on your CV. Some consultants — particularly at teaching hospitals — will not consider a future employee without one. By no means does this mean everyone should do one — remember, only *some* consultants think this way. The year is often self-funded and thus can be expensive; also, you may not be interested in science and may not wish to watch your friends progressing with their careers while you stagnate at university for *another* year.

Those of you with a morbid passion for science (or a masochistic streak) may progress after your BSc to study for a PhD qualification, the postgraduate science degree. There are an increasing number of intercalated PhD courses available as part of an MB,PhD programme, for example at UCL. Funding is available for these courses but it is getting more competitive. The course involves combining the clinical course and studying for a PhD in the space of five years, which taken separately would amount to at least six years. Total time at medical school is, therefore, eight years (and you thought five was long!), graduating with a BSc, MB BS or equivalent and PhD furnishing you with the potential to progress into medical research at a later date.

Clinical course

This period is basically your apprenticeship on the wards. You ceremonially shave and exchange your scabby student clothes for more refined day wear and step out sporting your spanking new white coat, developing your skills of 'getting in the way' at nurses stations. Yes, yet again you are at the bottom of the pile (although you do get used to it). You are attached to 'firms' or teams within specialties for a few weeks learning the theory and clinical skills relevant to each and, just when you think you have grasped the concept, you are catapulted into an entirely new subject in which you are, once more, clueless. The specialties range from the elemental general medicine and surgery through the specialties of obstetrics and gynaecology, psychiatry, paediatrics, epidemiology, general practice (primary care) and many others. The bookwork continues, however, with further study in the disciplines of clinical pathology and pharmacology.

During the firms, you are given the opportunity to go 'on take' which means spending the night on call with your team in Accident and Emergency (A&E). Here you will see people suffering from acute and sometimes life-threatening illnesses — eg trauma, cardiac arrests, epileptic fits, acute asthma and meningitis. You will also sample the best that the local curry houses and pizza joints have to offer. This is a valuable time to learn and is also an opportunity to collar your bleary-eyed registrar for some impromptu teaching.

At the end of each firm, you are assessed on your knowledge and clinical skills, the latter focusing on taking the patients' story (history) and performing the physical/mental examination relevant to that discipline (known as 'clerking a patient'). You will be graded on the presentation of your findings and your ability to extract the relevant details and elicit the signs. Clinical assessment is increasingly being made using the Objective Structured Clinical Examination (OSCE). Here you rotate every three minutes or so around different 'stations' where clinicians examine you on your knowledge and clinical skills, for example passing a baby through a pelvis, counselling a patient (often performed by harrowingly realistic actors), taking a blood pressure etc.

> *In A&E, you will see people suffering from acute and life-threatening illnesses (eg trauma, cardiac arrests)*

In the fourth or fifth year, you have the opportunity to travel to a hospital of your choice (or one that will have you) almost anywhere in the world for about eight weeks for your elective period. Ask any doctor about their elective period and they will slip into a trance and fondly reminisce about the sun-kissed, white-sanded beaches of Australia, gunshot wounds in Chicago or the diarrhoea in Singapore airport. The potential for variety is immense. You can pursue a specialty of your choice or link it to a personal interest; one colleague of mine went to NASA to look at astronautical medicine, another went to the US to study chaos theory as applied to medicine — I heard of one person who went to Beverly Hills, US, to expose himself to plastic surgery. Grants are available to help fund these ventures that often involve a project or a written report to the funding body afterwards.

At the end of three years, you sit your final examinations. There are written examinations based on multiple choice questions (MCQs) and essays in medicine (including paediatrics, psychiatry, epidemiology and public health), surgery (including orthopaedics, ear, nose and throat (ENT) and ophthalmology), obstetrics and gynaecology, pathology, and clinical pharmacology and therapeutics. There are also clinical examinations in these subjects that may become more OSCE-orientated in the future, but currently consist of clerking and presentation of a long case and short cases in front of two examiners and a ritualistic grilling by two further examiners in the oral examination or viva. Success in these gets you a medical degree.

There is no grading in medicine — you either pass or fail. Naturally, there are distinctions and prizes to be won that will shine on your CV, however, one-upmanship will get you nowhere. If you pass, it is because *you* make the mark, not because everyone else is less intelligent. It is worth remembering when the compulsory year crawler tries to stab you in the back to make themselves look good.

Playtime

The take-home message from this section is whatever you want to do, whatever you can afford to do in cash and time, there is probably the opportunity to do it at medical school. You make your own choices, find your own crowd and play your own games.

All UK medical schools are now linked to universities and have a vast array of societies that you can join; if they do not and you have the support, the facilities are available for you to form your own. Your life does not, and in my view should not, stop at university. Many of you will find yourself in an entirely new city, with all its associated benefits eg the local mountain range, the nightclubs, bands looking for new members, charities etc.

The medical school community seems insular to many. However, these are the people you will not only be studying with, but they will eventually qualify too. It can be a relief (but sometimes a shock) to see a familiar face in a hospital you find yourself working in. There are various traditions that continue with strength: rag week, an all-in effort for charity (from the traditional bed push to hitch-hikes to Amsterdam); Christmas and summer balls and other formal dinners (often memorable, some best forgotten, others simply can't be recalled); medical school revues (no, really, they *can* be funny), and of course the various medical school sports teams. Intermedical school sports events are among the most aggressively fought conflicts, and vigorous celebrations can result. The classic sports teams still are important: rugby, hockey (slightly,

but only just slightly more classy), football, rowing (early starters, invariably dull), netball, volleyball, water polo and many more. Wednesday afternoons are currently free to enable you to follow your chosen pursuits. The only reason for going to the library at this time should be to catch up on the backlog of work you have amassed while going out on other occasions, or during the examination period.

Examinations

There is no substitute, I am afraid, for work in passing examinations. However, effective work is important. Taking out a mortgage to buy all the textbooks in the shop so that every nugget of information passes into your head from the shelf by pure osmosis is senseless. If your proud Gran is about to rush out and pawn her dentures to buy you a copy of *Gray's Anatomy*, tell her to stay on solids until you have found a book *you* like. Any self-respecting medical school will have everything you need in the library to pass your examinations, so use it.

MCQ examinations are a cruel basis for assessment favoured by sadistic tutors based on your ability to know whether or not a zillion facts thrown at you in an hour are true or false. If you get one right, then you get one mark but woe-betide a false answer as that will take one mark away. Thus, to obtain 50% (the pass-mark) and you answer all the questions, you need to get 75% of the answers correct. These types of examinations are best passed by practising until you bleed, so get past-papers or sample questions from your colleagues, or swap them for your Gran if she has run out of pawnable prostheses, as these are gold-dust. Please feel free to beat up the lonely crawler who keeps the past-papers to themselves with my blessing — remember what I said about making your mark irrespective of other people's performance? Lack of knowledge or foolish over-confidence can be your ruin. Find out which you suffer from and amend your skill appropriately. You will see your marks improve with time.

This principle applies for all examinations — practice writing essays, see as many patients as you can, and ensure your history-taking, examination and subsequent presentation are comprehensive and slick and you will be fine. There are lots of revision texts out there — we all used them and found them extremely helpful. Try not to cram; remember, what you learn has to stay in your head after you qualify if you are to be any use at all, so consistent work throughout the course will stand you in good stead for the run up to any examination.

Survival

My only bit of advice for surviving medical school is know your capabilities and organize your time accordingly. Do not be corrupted by your clever, but annoying, friends who go out all the time, casually sniff a textbook two minutes before an examination and obtain a distinction. If you need to work harder to pass, then work harder. This may seem obvious, but much of the learning you will do will be during your free time and it is entirely self-motivated; trust me, I know, self-discipline can be tricky when temptation is scratching at your door whispering *'beer and curry, beer and curry'* (or whatever it is that tempts you). I know I sound like my Dad, but if you are set an essay, practical write-up or project, do not put it off, just *get it done* — if you let your work pile up, you will be up all hours producing poor-quality work at the end of term when everyone else is going out and enjoying themselves. It can be an even bigger shock when there are end of term examinations to worry about.

If you do the work you have been set, keep up with your subjects for revision and organize your time, you will be able to do the things *you* want to do, when *you* want to do them. You can make your timetable work for you and not vice versa.

Summary

You will leave medical school as a doctor after five, six or even eight years, with the essential skills to pursue a challenging and fulfilling career with diverse opportunities which will satisfy the most bizarre of appetites.

Although this chapter mainly covers the academic and social sides of medical school, remember that you will also be required to develop yourself as a person. You will be studying for a vocation where what you do affects people, their lives and whole families, not merely manipulating pathology specimens. Even as a student, what you say or do will make a difference. Sometimes when I imagine myself or my parents as the patient, I can be horrified by my lack of perspective. You work in a team that includes people from the vast range of disciplines within any hospital's employ. Listen to people, learn from them, admit your limitations and you will enjoy the job so much more.

Yes, it *is* worth it in the end and, if you have done it right, you will leave with a stack of memories so big you can bore your friends for years — so good luck!

Further reading

Bastyra J. *Making the most of being a student*. London: Kogan Page, 1998. (ISBN: 0749426411) (This is an excellent, accessible guide that covers everything from basic life skills, such as ironing a shirt and wiring a plug, to the more serious business of organizing your time and finances.)

Shem S. The house of God. London: Black Swan, 1985. (ISBN: 0552991228) (A semi-fictional account of the intern year at an American teaching hospital, written by a physician. Love it or loath it, many of us have read it before, or just after, qualifying and found the themes frighteningly familiar.)

The resident years

Dr Robina Coker, Hammersmith Hospital, London

9

This chapter aims to provide an insight into becoming and working as a medical registrar. In some respects, life as a medical registrar is similar to that of a surgical registrar, but different specialties obviously entail distinct working practices, skills, training and examinations. The chapter is based on my own experience in general and respiratory medicine, thus it cannot be a comprehensive guide to the resident years in all disciplines. Nevertheless, it is hoped that the reader will gain some impression of what is involved at this stage of one's career.

It is useful to have some idea of the training involved before becoming a registrar and I will begin with an outline of my own experience. Since I became a registrar, the Calman reforms have been introduced. These reforms aim to shorten the duration of registrar training, expand consultant numbers and harmonize specialist training requirements with the rest of the European Union. Future medical graduates will, therefore, probably experience more rapid career progression. However, the years at medical school are really only the beginning of a longer period of training as a junior hospital doctor, whether medical or surgical, before obtaining a hospital consultant appointment.

Training

Undergraduate training

In 1980, I entered St Thomas' Hospital Medical School, now united with Guy's and King's College Hospitals. After two years of a pre-clinical course composed of modules in anatomy, biochemistry, physiology, pharmacology, psychology and sociology, I obtained a Medical Research Council Scholarship to study for a BSc degree in pharmacology. In 1983, I completed my BSc course, which consisted of two terms working at St Thomas' and one term studying at University College London. I then rejoined students in the year below to complete three more years of clinical training. Most of this time was spent on the wards at St Thomas', but there were also attachments in hospitals outside London in various specialties, including paediatrics, general surgery and cardiology. I obtained my Bachelor of Medicine and Bachelor of Surgery (MB BS) qualification in 1986.

Postgraduate training

In August 1986, I began a pre-registration house officer post in surgery in Suffolk. I returned to London six months later as a pre-registration house officer in medicine at St Thomas'. By 1987, I had decided to pursue a career in hospital medicine. I, therefore, applied for SHO posts in medicine and studied for part I and, subsequently, part II of the examinations for Membership of the Royal College of Physicians (MRCP) of London. I obtained the MRCP in 1989 and was appointed to a three-year registrar rotation in general and chest medicine that started in early 1990. Three years later, I obtained funding to study for a PhD qualification and completed this period of laboratory research in 1996. I returned to full-time clinical medicine in 1997 and was appointed as senior registrar in general and chest medicine. In 1999, I obtained a consultant/senior lecturer post, which involves both hospital and university work.

This brief résumé demonstrates that the resident years are only part of a fairly long, although challenging and interesting, period of postgraduate training. The emphasis on research may not be so great in future years due to the changes introduced by the Calman reforms; however, a significant number of specialist registrars, certainly in medical specialties, are likely to take at least one year out for research, if not two or three. The specialist registrar period of training itself currently lasts five years. By the time postgraduates reach the beginning of these resident years, they will have completed five or six years at medical school, one year of pre-registration house officer posts

and two to three years of medical SHO posts — that is a minimum of eight years since entering medical school; this assumes no change of mind about speciality and no retaking of examinations. The latter cannot be guaranteed — the pass rate for the clinical examination in the part II MRCP examinations is about 30%. For women, this career choice has implications for those wishing to have a family. Part-time training is increasingly available but still not abundant. For those who find themselves in this position, I suggest you talk to at least one person in a similar situation who has already embarked on your chosen career pathway, and obtain a thorough picture of available options before you start. This is far better than starting out, realizing you have made the wrong choice, and then having to continue under difficult circumstances or trying to change career path.

Medical school is only the start of a longer training period as a junior hospital doctor before becoming a hospital consultant

Typical working week

The rest of this chapter aims to give the reader an idea of life as a medical registrar by detailing events in a typical week. Although based on fact, the characters described are fictitious.

Monday

The day begins with a social meeting at 9 o'clock. I arrive just in time and we begin discussion about the first patient. One disadvantage of the new Calman rotations is that hospitals within each rotation are often quite far from each other, entailing long travelling times from home — my present commute involves at least two hours daily. Driving after being on call and awake for most of the night can be difficult, but travelling by public transport in London takes longer and costs twice as much.

The social meeting is not a chance to catch up on the latest hospital gossip — it is an ideal opportunity to discuss patients as part of a multidisciplinary team. It generally includes at least one ward sister or staff nurse, the social worker, physiotherapist and occupational therapist for our two main wards (the male and female respiratory wards). In some hospitals, the team might also include a ward pharmacist, dietician and speech therapist. Owing to pressures on beds, we invariably have patients on outlying wards and it is a good chance to update the team on their progress. All the medical firms take part in the acute medical on-call rota, so we have our share of patients with general medical problems as well as those with respiratory disease. Multidisciplinary meetings are particularly useful for making decisions on how best to manage patients with chronic illness or difficult social circumstances; these include patients with strokes and chronic lung disease (Figure 1).

At about 9.30, we begin the consultant ward round. Our house officer, Claire, has produced a computerized record of patients listed by ward. There are 19 patients today and it takes us until midday to see all of them. Styles of ward round vary; some consultants like to discuss all patients on

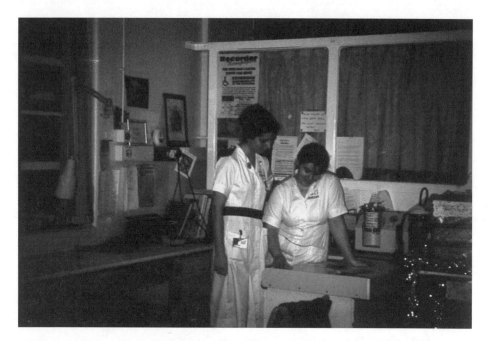

Figure 1 Nurses discuss a patient's management plan

each ward together at the beginning while others like to discuss the case-notes and progress at the bedside. Our house officer brings everyone up to date with latest developments and I contribute extra information as required. Our SHO is away this week on study leave for part II of the MRCP examinations, so I shall be extra busy on the wards in his absence. This particular ward round involves the consultant breaking bad news to a patient whom we have just found has lung cancer. I will have to talk to her relatives later as they were unable to visit this morning.

We finish the ward round at midday and I go back to one of the wards with Claire to help her insert a chest drain. This would usually be the SHO's job, but the hospital rarely provides locum cover for short-term leave, with the exception of on-call duties. This leaves us with time for a quick lunch in the hospital canteen. Claire goes off to start the tasks arising from the ward round and I give the medical students attached to our firm a one-hour teaching session. They have requested teaching on clinical cases, so I ask two of them to present a patient they have seen in the past week. We spend some time discussing them and I then take them to examine one of our patients with classic signs of a pleural effusion (accumulation of fluid in the pleural cavity).

At 3 o'clock, I go back to the registrars' office to work on my research project, which involves a national survey of chest consultant's views on the advice they give to patients with lung disease planning air travel. I am in the process of finishing the design of the questionnaire and will soon begin mailing them. At 4.30, I return to the ward to talk to the relatives of our newly diagnosed patient with lung cancer. Claire agrees to hold my bleep for half an hour so that we are not disturbed and I ask the ward nurse looking after the patient to join us. The family are understandably distressed and it takes us some time to discuss the possible treatments available. I then return to the registrar's office for an hour to dictate discharge summaries.

Tuesday

I have an outpatient clinic starting at 9 o'clock. Today there are 14 patients on the list, which is overbooked. However, they are all follow-up appointments, either for patients recently discharged from the ward or those with chronic problems under long-term follow-up. Since I know most of them reasonably well, the clinic should not last much longer than scheduled. As it happens, one of the patients is quite unwell with severe pneumonia. After telephoning the bed manager to locate an available bed, I arrange for admission to one of the medical wards and inform Claire that the patient needs to be assessed soon after his arrival on the ward. We arrange to review the patient together in the afternoon. This process delays me somewhat and I finish the clinic at 12.40 pm. I manage to grab a quick lunch in the postgraduate centre with the other medical registrars before attending the hospital grand round at 1 o'clock.

The grand round is very interesting. Following two case presentations, one of the intensive care consultants discusses the role of hyperbaric oxygen (the treatment of which involves administration of 100% oxygen in a high pressure chamber for gas gangrene and carbon monoxide poisoning). This hospital has one of only a few units in the country providing hyperbaric oxygen, and its therapeutic role is not generally well understood.

Immediately afterwards, I meet Claire to review the patient I admitted from clinic. He is beginning to respond to treatment, but I make a note to let the on-call registrar know about him before I leave this evening. After this, we start our ward round. Four patients were discharged yesterday and another two this morning; most of the others are either improving or are stable. However, there is one patient I am concerned about. He is in his late-40s and has suffered a stroke. We had expected him to have a brain scan yesterday but the radiology department was overbooked and his condition has deteriorated since we saw him yesterday. We interrupt the ward round to visit the radiology department and find one of the consultants, who agrees to perform an urgent computed tomography (CT) scan early this evening. I add him to my list to hand over to the on-call team.

Once the ward round is finished, I return to the office to find a pile of laboratory results on my desk that need to be checked before filing. I discover that an outpatient seen at the end of last week is over-anticoagulated and manage to telephone him at home. I give him advice about what dose reduction he should make, and we agree he will come up to the hospital again in two days' time for another blood test. I leave the request form with our secretary who will give it to him when he calls in. Before leaving, I bleep the on-call medical registrar and tell her about my patient who is having the urgent CT brain scan and the one with pneumonia. She agrees to review both in the course of the evening.

Wednesday

Wednesday begins with another ward round with Claire. When the wards are quiet, I often let our SHO do this ward round. Today is fairly busy — our stroke patient has stabilized overnight and his CT scan showed no indication to transfer him to a neurosurgical unit. However, his family are understandably very anxious and I spend some time with them answering their queries. The patient with pneumonia is making good progress. Yesterday's on-call team has returned two patients to our care. One is a lady with fairly advanced lung cancer well known to our firm and another is a man with severe chronic bronchitis; the former needs careful assessment and the latter requires some changes in treatment.

At midday, I manage to leave the wards and walk over to the endoscopy suite for the bronchoscopy list. Bronchoscopy examination enables you to visualize the larynx, trachea and bronchi; a long, flexible fibre-optic tube is introduced through nose or mouth. There are four patients on the list today, but the consultant has already seen two of them so I am able to attend to the remaining two and grab a sandwich before the afternoon clinic. I enjoy the bronchoscopy list — practical procedures are very satisfying and most of the patients are relieved to find the procedure is not as traumatic as they had feared.

The outpatients list starts at 2.00 pm and is a busy cardiology clinic. I am specializing in chest medicine, but there is a longstanding interdepart-mental agreement that one of the chest registrars will help out. It is a while since I did a specialist cardiology post and, as I do not usually work for this consultant, I ask his opinion fairly frequently. The clinic finishes at 5.40 pm and it takes me until 6.00 pm to dictate the letters and arrange a few outstanding investigations.

Thursday

We begin with a consultant ward round at 9.30. I peel off after half an hour to do a clinic list for one of the other chest consultants. In this clinic, I usually see one or two new patients, which provides good experience in making decisions about appropriate investigations and management. At 12.30 pm, I attend our departmental X-ray meeting over a sandwich. This is informal and usually lasts about one hour. It is an excellent opportunity to discuss clinical problems and review patients' radiology. Afterwards, I run through the patient list with Claire. There are two patients she is concerned about, so we go and see them together. I then return to the registrars' office to dictate discharge summaries and finish printing 350 copies of my survey questionnaire and covering letter.

Friday

Friday begins at 8 o'clock with a meeting in the chest clinic for the three consultants and two registrars. It is informal and provides an opportunity to present and discuss interesting or problematic patients. At 9 o'clock, Claire and I begin the ward round, and finish by spending time with some relatives. I manage a civilized lunch today in the postgraduate centre. In the afternoon, we have the chest clinic meeting. This involves all three chest teams and the respiratory nurses and lung function technicians. This afternoon one of the consultants discusses the introduction of the new CFC-inhalers for asthma. There is plenty of time for discussion afterwards. Later, I return to the office to finish off paperwork.

Saturday

Saturday I am on call for acute general medicine. We begin at 9 o'clock by checking that the team are all present. Claire is not on call today, and our

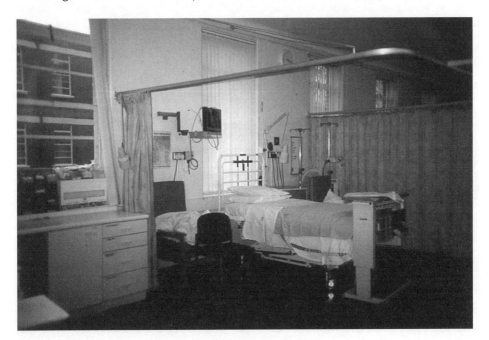

Figure 2   A bed on the CCU with overhead cardiac monitor

SHO is replaced by a locum who is new to the hospital. I have not worked with the first on-call house officer before either, so we agree a fairly detailed plan of how we will work together in casualty. The second on-call house officer will cover the wards and only bleep me if worried. As we begin the coronary care unit (CCU) ward round, the sister from casualty bleeps me to let me know that there is a referral for us from the casualty team. I send the SHO to clerk the patient. Meanwhile, I continue the CCU round, which takes about 45 minutes. The patients are stable with the exception of a 42-year-old man, who is getting frequent angina despite near-maximal treatment. There are no facilities in this hospital for coronary angiography (which involves passing a fine catheter into the heart and examining coronary arteries under X-ray screening after injecting a radio-opaque contrast medium) or surgery, and he may need emergency ambulance transfer to the regional cardiothoracic centre. Sister and I agree on which patients are fit enough to be transferred to a general ward, which leaves me with two beds available for new admissions (Figure 2). I leave the house officer to rewrite drug charts and go to casualty. We now have two more referrals waiting, and the morning looks to be busy. The SHO sees all the patients first unless he is particularly worried about their condition, and I review them when the immediate blood, X-ray and electrocardiogram results are available. By lunchtime we have admitted five patients.

Figure 3 Ambulance staff bring a patient to Accident & Emergency

As we are finishing lunch, the cardiac arrest bleeps go off and we are called to one of the medical wards. The patient is successfully resuscitated but will need admission to intensive care. I spend over an hour sorting out immediate management and speaking to the family. Fortunately, we still have intensive care beds available this weekend, or we would have to arrange emergency transfer to another unit.

I return to casualty. By the end of the afternoon we have admitted eight patients (Figure 3). Three were referred by their general practitioners and two were sent home by us, with urgent outpatient appointments to be made next week. My list of Monday jobs is growing. I review the CCU patient with angina. His symptoms have settled. I decide, following discussion with the registrar on call at our nearest cardiothoracic unit, not to transfer him but continue the same treatment.

The evening is relatively quiet. We decide to order pizza as a change from supper in the hospital canteen and manage to eat it together in the doctors' mess. Then a further stream of casualty referrals begins and the three of us get down to work. By midnight, most tasks are complete. A further four patients admitted have been clerked (see page 49) and treatment begun, and the second on-call house officer tells me the wards are quiet. Only the results from a lumbar puncture (sampling of the cerebrospinal fluid under local anaesthetic) are outstanding. The first on-call house officer will make sure they are available for review with the SHO before he goes to bed. I go to bed, leaving the SHO to finish sorting out two more patients accompanied by relatives whom we have agreed can go home.

At 2.25 am my bleep goes off. It is the SHO on call for the care of the elderly firm. He is worried about a patient who has developed septic shock and does not have enough experience to insert a central intravenous catheter. It is my job to cover this team when on-call at night, so I agree to help. It takes me some time to sort out this patient, who is seriously ill, and I ask the intensive therapy unit (ITU) registrar to see her. He is busy on the orthopaedic wards and does not manage to see the patient until 4 am. We agree on a management plan to be reviewed first thing in the morning, and I talk to the nurses about which observations will be needed. They move the patient closer to the nurses' desk where they can monitor her more readily. At 4.40 I get to bed again, and my alarm goes off at 7.30 for the 8 o'clock morning ward round.

During the night, the SHO has admitted three more patients, so we now have 15 in total. This is a relatively small number and is likely to increase substantially in the winter months, as will the pressure on beds. The consultant ward round, which includes a check on the progress of the care of the elderly patient, finishes just before 11 o'clock. I spend another half an hour making sure the SHO and house officer know which jobs must be done before they hand over to today's on-call team. I then contact today's on-call registrar to hand him the cardiac arrest bleep and let him know about two patients who are quite ill and need review later today. I drive home more slowly than usual after my interrupted night's sleep, and open the front door at 12.10. Saturday's *British Medical Journal* lies inside on the doormat. It is time for lunch and a leisurely afternoon before starting another week tomorrow morning.

Choosing general practice (primary care)   **10**

Dr Edward Shaoul, Associate Dean, St Charles' Hospital, London

This chapter will discuss the entry requirements for general practice (primary care), and will focus on what this branch of medicine can offer you and what opportunities are made available from it.

Medical school entry

If you already feel a strong vocation towards general practice (primary care) and wish to say so at your selection interview, there is no harm in doing so. These days, general practitioners (GPs) sit on many interview panels and it will be recognized by the interviewers that the initial aspirations of most candidates will change in the course of their career.

The medical school curriculum is as comprehensive as possible. There will be many opportunities to see most specialties, including general practice (primary care), in the course of the five or six years that you will be at medical school, and many undergraduates become tempted by what they see changing in a positive and healthy way throughout their undergraduate years. However, about 60% of all undergraduates in medicine will make a career in general practice (primary care) for a variety of reasons.

Reasons for choosing general practice (primary care)

There is an opportunity to see a wide range of conditions in which you will be the first-in-line doctor, which can be very exciting. More than 90% of patients who consult a GP will be managed and treated within the primary care setting. You will have the opportunity to provide continuity of care and be able to see the progress or cure of a particular condition. You will form a relationship within the community in which you work and will enjoy independence as a self-employed practitioner who, in fact, will employ staff to work with him.

A few practitioners choose to be employed within a small organization setting; it seems likely that about 30% of GPs will choose this route in the future. However, as a self-employed doctor, you will be able to exercise more control over the hours of work, allowing considerable freedom with

> *You will reach a responsible status earlier and have the opportunity to work longer than those in hospital specialties*

the organization of family life — this is particularly helpful to those doctors in the child-bearing years.

The entrance conditions are shorter and less arduous than for many other specialties. As a result, you will reach a responsible status earlier and will have the opportunity to work longer so that your life long earnings will be comparable with those doctors who choose to go into a hospital specialty.

There will be ample opportunity for you to become an expert in a particular field if you wish to do so, and to temper the work that you do with patients with other activities — this may be professional or non-professional.

General practice (primary care) entry

The basic medical degree and hospital officer posts are common to all branches of medicine. Undergraduates who have attained and developed a broad view are more likely to be successful in entering general practice (primary care) training schemes. Do not be frightened to continue to practice your music, develop your dramatic skills, work abroad in medicine for a short period of time or spend a year doing a research post.

Once you have completed your registration, you can at any time apply for a three-year rotation for general practice (primary care) called the vocational training scheme — which will guarantee a complete training package without needing to find a new hospital post every six months — or a general practice (primary care) registrarship. Most of these posts are at senior house officer (SHO) level and are usually based at one hospital. There will be a special training programme for general practice (primary care) in addition to the specialty teaching programme.

It is possible to build your own scheme by choosing four SHO posts and finding a general practice (primary care) registrarship yourself. However, this route is likely to become harder to achieve in the future, although many excellent GPs have chosen to organize their training in this way. Entry requirements for such a scheme vary from an application form and interview to a pre-application MCQ paper followed by an exhausting, but exciting, extended interview process; in the latter, candidates are selected not only for their potential for general practice (primary care) but also for their ability to work within the training group.

General practice (primary care) training is well organized and well monitored. The hospital posts and general practice (primary care) training posts are selected with great care and are constantly supervised. The programme is run at a local level by a course organizer who will work at a personal level with all doctors on the scheme.

To complete the training period, doctors must pass a course work examination called Summative Assessment, which tests their clinical knowledge and skills together with their consultation skills. This is set at a minimal competence level so that any doctor who has been admitted to the training course, and applies himself diligently, should be able to pass.

An alternative assessment by examination for Membership of the Royal College of General Practitioner is also available.

Work involved in general practice (primary care)

What do GPs do? Why is it exciting? Is it financially rewarding? What other benefits are there? These questions are answered in this section.

The patients you see as a GP are not selected by another professional. You find your day is made up of a mix of very common and extremely rare conditions. This requires you to possess very highly refined diagnostic skills and to be able to recognize small differences between apparently similar presentations. You will have ample opportunity to use a variety of personal skills in areas such as psychiatry, manipulation, skin conditions, surgical conditions and eye examinations, and you will be able to recognize your particular skills and interests and have the opportunity to expand such skills.

You will be in a unique position to view the whole patient and understand any underlying problems, not just necessarily make a clinical diagnosis. Not only will you work with indi-
vidual patients, but also with their families who may be registered with you. You will be able to see patients as frequently as you think necessary, you will be able to visit them at their home and they will feel able and comfortable to approach you in a non-formal manner. You will, thus, be able to develop

knowledge of the whole family structure, which may include anything up to five generations of one family. You will witness family life events such as births, marriages and, sadly, deaths.

In addition to your day-to-day contact with your patients, you will have ample opportunity from general practice (primary care) to develop related interests. These may be: academic interests, helping to teach undergraduates and postgraduates the various skills of general practice (primary care); being involved in research, either on your own or as part of a team; developing an interest in forensic medicine, such as police work; or choosing to make an in-depth study of family dynamics and family medicine. Some of you will use general practice (primary care) as a base to develop your interests in occupational health. A few of you will develop such skills and interests and will continue to do either one or two hospital sessions per week in certain specialties, such as dermatology and psychiatry and accident and emergency. Most of these additional interests will carry a financial reward.

General practice (primary care) versus hospital medicine

You have to admit that general practice (primary care) sounds very exciting and stimulating, but, for example, how does the pay compare to that of specialist colleagues? It is important to remember that GPs start earning a full income sooner than their hospital colleagues will, and can also work to the age of 70 years and need not retire at the age of 65. As the hospital training programme is about four to seven years longer and there is the opportunity to work for the five years between their 65th and 70th birthday, the life time earnings of general practice (primary care) receive a considerable boost. GPs are expected to earn about £53,000/year plus expenses, totalling about £78,000/year, whereas a hospital doctor at the top of their scale will be earning about £67,000/year. Some hospital specialists will develop a lucrative private practice and there is no denying that those who work very hard will achieve extremely high levels of earning. Many hospital specialists will be able, at some time in their career, to receive a boost to their income called the merit award but there is no equivalent scheme for general practice (primary care). However, they have the opportunity to invest in their surgery premises at favourable rates, and many GPs find that they are able to make a capital gain when they come to retire from general practice (primary care). The financial issues in general practice (primary care) and hospital medicine are summarized in Table 1.

Hospital doctors are employed by the Health Service Trust for which they work. The Trust will provide them with a fixed income and will be responsible for the equipment they use and the staff they have to support them. They will also expect the doctors they employ to be managed by managers

Table 1   Finances: general practice (primary care) versus hospital medicine

GP	Hospital specialist
• Starts earning sooner	• Training takes longer — about 7–10 years
• Can work to the age of 70 years	• Retire at the age of 65 years
• Review body pay: £43,000 plus expenses; can expect to earn c£65,000/yr	• Can expect to earn c£67,000/yr; may develop lucrative private practice

employed by the Health Service Trust. The structure in general practice (primary care) is very different. The contract offered by the health authority to GPs is fixed centrally and can be changed by the government arbitrarily. Nevertheless, GPs remain independent contractors and can choose their level of work and the patients for whom they wish to be responsible. Freedom of choice in the management of certain conditions is possible. Although some doctors will choose to provide care for drug addicts on their list, others may decide that this is not an aspect of general practice (primary care) they enjoy and exclude such care from their contract.

There is also an opportunity to vary the length of the working week in general practice (primary care) and, because of their independence, GPs can rearrange their workload within the practice, can organize their holidays, choose their professional partners and, very importantly, choose the staff they wish to employ. Many practitioners own the premises in which they work and, in recognizing the importance of satisfactory working conditions for general practice (primary care), the Department of Health have a number of supportive financial schemes to enable practices to build new premises and renovate old premises.

It is important to understand that all branches of medicine are challenging and if you are in doubt as to whether or not you can meet these demands, it is probably better not to start. In addition, you should be aware that you can succeed in any branch of medicine you choose if you want to. You will change your mind several times on the way through medical school and in the early years of your career — some doctors even change their minds much later on. Between 50 and 60% of all entrants will become GPs.

Types of practice

Single-handed practice

Some doctors who enter general practice (primary care) do not enjoy working in partnership with other doctors for a variety of reasons. This is very often due to a financial dispute that has arisen in a previous partnership arrangement. It may also be because the doctor concerned has found it difficult to find colleagues with whom they can work and prefer the ease of decision-making involved in working single-handed. No long practice meetings for them and no need to bend their wishes to those of other partners. However, a disadvantage to working in a single-handed practice is that you are isolated, both professionally and in the provision of cover for absence. There are many ways of overcoming this disadvantage and many single-handed practitioners work in close cooperation with other single-handed practitioners to obtain some of the benefits of working together without the administrative difficulties that arise from partnerships.

Partnership

Most GPs will work in partnership and the trend over the past 10 years has been for these partnerships to become bigger and bigger. By pooling resources, these practices are able to buy equipment needed to help in their daily work and to employ a practice manager to help to take some of the administrative burden off their shoulders. They are also often able to have a wider variety of practice staff working with them and to be able to host educational meetings within their premises.

Health centres

A few practices will choose to work from Health Service-owned premises called health centres. They are spared the financial responsibility for the building from which they work, and have the benefit of working in close proximity with other healthcare workers employed by the community trust but not by the practice. But many practitioners have learnt that the quality of these buildings often leaves a lot to be desired, and the maintenance often requires protracted negotiation with the financially restricted Health Authority that is responsible for maintaining them. So most practitioners prefer to work from modern, privately developed premises for which they receive considerable financial support from the Health Service, but yet the partners retain the independence that comes from owning the building, together with the opportunities to make a capital gain in later life.

Location of practice

Where do doctors choose to practice? As partners, these can be divided into three distinct areas. Some doctors will choose to run a long way away from the cities and to set up practice in a rural area. Although these are often geographically very desirable and provide an excellent quality of life, they can be very demanding, requiring a high level of interventional skills to compensate for the distance to the nearest hospital, and there are difficulties of professional isolation because of the distance between the various doctors who are working together.

In contrast, some doctors may choose to work in an inner city practice where the entire practice population is within half a mile. In these practices, you would need to meet the challenges of a multiracial society, bringing with it language difficulties, a very mobile, and often very specialized, population such as a refugee population or an ethnic group. This is compensated for by being near hospitals and, often, close to teaching hospitals with ample opportunities to learn new skills and to be heavily involved in the teaching of undergraduate students from those hospitals.

Somewhere between these two extremes are the suburban practices working in the leafy suburbs, often with very comfortable premises, not too far from the main hospitals and with an excellent community relationship with their local hospital — many doctors opt to work in such an area. However, nothing is completely idyllic and patients living in these areas are often very demanding and cause the doctors a considerable amount of frustration.

Increasingly, we are now finding that many younger doctors are choosing not to commit themselves to a life-long attachment to a particular practice. They are not opting to go into partnership, but rather to work within those practices as assistants or as salaried principals. These doctors will earn less money and will not be entitled to the tax advantages of being self-employed, but they will often find the comfort of having a guaranteed income adequate compensation for this. What I have tried to show you is that the opportunities that exist are very varied.

Typical working day in general practice (primary care)

What is a day in general practice (primary care) like? What is the nature of the work? Why do I find it attractive and so rewarding? I will outline my typical day to help answer these questions and to give an insight into general practice (primary care).

The day starts with morning surgery. In addition to the patients who have made appointments, there will usually be an extra three or four who feel their condition so urgent that they cannot wait for the next surgery. Some of these patients will have a minor problem that can easily be dismissed by reassurance or confirmation of a simple diagnosis such as mumps or chicken pox. Occasionally among these extra patients, there will be one that constitutes a real emergency, which could be a severe asthma attack, a heart attack or bleeding from somewhere in the gastrointestinal tract. You will be faced with the difficulty of dealing with this emergency, knowing that those patients who have booked a routine appointment will inevitably be seen later than they had expected. Nevertheless, the satisfactory management of the emergency not only helps the patient concerned but also gives the doctor considerable satisfaction. Perhaps not so surprisingly, the patients who were delayed in the waiting room are usually very understanding and grateful that it was not their emergency with which you were having to deal.

The variety in the morning surgery will be infinite. A few of the patients will be routine monitoring procedures such as reasonably well-controlled hypertension or diabetes, but every so often one patient will be completely out of control and all your skill will be needed. You may well be within a small influenza epidemic and seeing half a dozen patients with coughs, colds and bad chests and yet you will have the responsibility of picking out among those patients the one who has tuberculosis or cancer of the lung. Some of the patients may need to be taught how to use their inhaler for the management of their asthma. Although you may choose to do this yourself, you may also have the opportunity to pass this patient to your practice nurse who will be very skilled at teaching the breathing technique necessary for the asthma device they use.

A patient may present with recurring headaches. You will be aware from the knowledge of the family of a number of background problems to be overcome in order to resolve the symptoms. You will then call in the next patient. Their face will be all smiles as they come to thank you for correctly diagnosing the lump in their breast as having been a very early cancer that had been successfully removed at the local breast clinic giving the patient a clean bill of health.

At the end of the morning surgery, I may well go on to run my antenatal clinic in conjunction with one of the midwives from the local hospital. Some of the mothers that I will be examining will be the very babies that I delivered at home or in a hospital unit 25 years ago. Other mothers will be new to me and I will need to establish with them the strong family links that I consider being important to my style of practice. An antenatal clinic is very different from morning surgery. The patients are well, they are happy, they are a little bit anxious but easily reassured and it is great fun demonstrating to them the various bits of the baby's anatomy that can be felt through the abdominal wall. They have many questions to ask but somehow this never seems to be a chore. The morning is all too short and it is already time to stop for lunch.

Sometimes lunch will mean jumping in the car and driving to a meeting and eating sandwiches while matters of Health Service administration are discussed at one committee or another, or perhaps the teaching of medical students for the forthcoming term. Sometimes lunch is meeting with the partners and perhaps part of the practice team to discuss the running of the practice itself. Sometimes lunch is a personal affair with nothing to disturb the flow of digestive juices.

I find nowadays that I can very rarely do any home visits in the morning, so I will plan to do these in the afternoon. Most visits these days will involve seeing patients who have no mobility at all. Many patients now come to the practice. However, one group of patients that I do choose to visit at home are mothers who have just had a baby. I find that it helps considerably in the development of a close relationship between the practice and the mothers, and it gives me an opportunity to meet them in their home surroundings where they can proudly show me their baby. I can answer their many questions about the management of this new member of their family. I will then go back to the surgery and read the not inconsiderable quantity of mail that has arrived and make decisions on the results of pathological tests that have been returned to me. I may have discussions with the district nurses or the practice nurses about procedures that need to be carried out and will then start the evening surgery which, in many ways, will be similar to the morning surgery although the mix of patients and the pace of the surgery is often very different. At the end of the day, I will ensure that all the actions that I needed to take for that day have been completed and go home.

It used to be that going home meant going home to be on duty for the practice. However, with the advent of cooperative organizations between many GPs we can now go home and expect to be undisturbed. Most GPs now participate in a cooperative emergency cover rota. Perhaps once a month or even less frequently than that, they will carry the responsibility for all the doctors who have signed up to that cooperative scheme. Although this change in working pattern is relatively recent, it became inevitable with the increasing workload in the daytime. Also, the increasing demands of patients for out of hour attention coupled with an increasing expectation of young practitioners for a more satisfactory quality of family life, which they found they were having difficulty in protecting, led to this change.

Is it worthwhile?

It is probably true to say that every day that I work in my surgery there will be at least one event that leads me to say 'I am glad that I went to work today and was able to do something to help a particular patient'. You certainly do not get up in the morning looking for that gratification but, nevertheless, when it happens it increases the fun of general practice (primary care).

Further reading

Humphries J, Brown L. *Careers in medicine, dentistry and mental health*. London: Kogan Page, 1996.

Richards P, Stockill S. *Learning medicine*. London: *BMJ* Publishing Group, 2000.

Brewster B, Mills J. *The doctor*. London: BBC, 1991.

RCGP careers information pack; can be obtained from 14 Princes Gate, Hyde Park, London SW7 1PU or http://www.rcgp.org.uk.

Choosing hospital medicine

Mr Kevin Lafferty, *Consultant Surgeon, Basildon Hospital, Essex*

The word 'hospital' is derived from the Latin 'hospes', meaning a guest, hence hospitality for the sick and poor. An average UK hospital cares for a population of 300,000 and employs about 2,000 people, of which around one-quarter are doctors and nurses. Ancillary and support workers include kitchen staff, porters, managers, engineers, gardeners, accountants, pharmacists, drivers, telephonists, secretaries and countless others. In many ways, a hospital resembles a small, self-sufficient community with each member holding a degree of responsibility for the success or failure of the whole.

Types of hospitals

Not all hospitals are the same. Teaching hospitals help with the training of medical students. District general hospitals provide a wide range of services to a local population. Hospitals such as Great Ormond Street Hospital for Sick Children serve a limited section of the community and provide specialized services. Private hospitals cater for private patients, who are usually seen and treated by consultants of the National Health Service (NHS) in addition to their normal NHS commitments.

Entering hospital medicine

The ultimate aim of a doctor embarking on a hospital career is a consultant post. Having finished medical school at about the age of 23, you must undertake a mandatory year as a pre-registration house officer (six months medicine and six months surgery) before officially joining the Medical Register. From there, it is a steady progression up through the ranks of different specialties.

The first step is a senior house officer post, which rotates at six-monthly intervals through different jobs within the broad spectrum of either medicine or surgery until about the age of 27. During this period, or earlier, you will decide on which aspect of hospital medicine interests you most. From age 27 until your mid-30s, you will undertake training as a specialist registrar in your chosen field, and can expect to become a consultant any time from about the age of 35 years onwards.

Why does entry take so long?

There is a great amount to learn — five years in medical school is only the beginning. Once you have qualified as a doctor, you must pass a series of postgraduate examinations before you can be entered on the register as an accredited specialist, whether for example in medicine, surgery, paediatrics or anaesthesia. Depending on your choice, you will face about three sets of examinations. All are difficult and are expensive to sit, and there is a high failure rate — many people fail at their first attempt.

In addition, gaining the necessary experience and maturity to practice independently as a consultant takes time. How soon will depend on your commitment and determination.

Choices in hospital medicine

Hospital medicine offers a wonderful variety of areas in which you can choose to specialize — a few are summarized below:

◎ brain, eyes, ENT (ears, nose and throat), head and neck
◎ chest and heart
◎ stomach and bowel
◎ liver, pancreas, kidneys and spleen
◎ bone and muscle, genital tract, breast
◎ blood vessels, skin, hormones
◎ trauma, rehabilitation.

There are also the 'ologys'. *Microbiology* is the study of germs — bacteria and viruses. *Pathology* studies tissues, which is important in diagnosing diseases such as cancer. *Radiology* is not simply the science of diagnosis using X-rays; radiologists are increasingly performing curative operations and procedures in their own right (interventional radiology). *Anesthesiology* (US spelling) is the technique of putting people to sleep for operations, but anaesthetists (UK spelling) are also branching out into other areas, such as the management of chronic pain.

Traditionally, those who specialize in pure medicine, known as physicians, have been arch rivals of surgeons, sometimes known as 'cutters'. But the truth is that these two branches of medicine, and those in between, are mutually dependent. In fact, the differences between the two groups are becoming increasingly blurred. These days, even some serious heart problems requiring attention can be treated by a cardiologist (physician) or a radiologist in a 10-minute procedure under X-ray control. Cardiac surgeons undertake the larger procedures involving open heart surgery for valves and coronary bypass operations. In 10–20 years, the boundaries between traditional physicians and surgeons will, however, become even more indistinct, and will probably disappear completely.

> *Hospital medicine can provide a lifetime of clinical interest, enjoyment, and the gratitude of patients*

Upside of hospital medicine

What are the upsides to a hospital career? It can provide a lifetime of clinical interest, enjoyment, and the gratitude of patients. There is much job satisfaction to be gained, and the money is good (about £60–70,000/year for a consultant, and a thriving private practice can double or treble this). The job commands respect and many hospital doctors attain an international reputation. In years to come, your grandchildren will be able to look up that celebrated paper or book you once wrote!

Downside of hospital medicine

In addition to long hours that keep you away from your family — often unpredictably — there can be a heavy burden of committee work and administration. The comparatively early death of many consultants has been attributed by the stress and long hours. Many hospital doctors retire early through ill health, because the job and the commitment required is so gruelling. Divorce and alcohol addiction is also higher than average. Patient expectations, particularly in this era of the empowered health consumer, can be extremely demanding. Depression and suicide rates are also higher than those of the general population. These problems are unlikely to be reduced in the present climate of professional governance and litigation.

Is it worth it?

The advantages and disadvantages are not much different from any other professional career — is it worth it? If you like people, enjoy being part of a team and want a lifetime interest in a field of your choice that enthuses you, the answer must be YES!

NOTES